T0098655

7 Mindsets *of* Success

7
Mindsets
of Success

*WHAT YOU REALLY NEED TO
DO TO ACHIEVE RAPID,
TOP-LEVEL SUCCESS*

STEN MORGAN

NEW YORK

NASHVILLE • MELBOURNE • VANCOUVER

7 Mindsets *of* Success
What You Really Need To Do To Achieve Rapid, Top-Level Success

© 2017 **STEN MORGAN**

All rights reserved. No portion of this book may be reproduced, stored in a retrieval system, or transmitted in any form or by any means—electronic, mechanical, photocopy, recording, scanning, or other,—except for brief quotations in critical reviews or articles, without the prior written permission of the publisher.

Published in New York, New York, by Morgan James Publishing. Morgan James is a trademark of Morgan James, LLC. www.MorganJamesPublishing.com

The Morgan James Speakers Group can bring authors to your live event. For more information or to book an event visit The Morgan James Speakers Group at www.TheMorganJamesSpeakersGroup.com.

ISBN 978-1-68350-301-9 paperback
ISBN 978-1-68350-303-3 eBook
ISBN 978-1-68350-302-6 hardcover
Library of Congress Control Number: 2016917103

Cover Design by:
Chris Treccani
www.3dogdesign.net

Interior Design by:
Bonnie Bushman
The Whole Caboodle Graphic Design

In an effort to support local communities, raise awareness and funds, Morgan James Publishing donates a percentage of all book sales for the life of each book to Habitat for Humanity Peninsula and Greater Williamsburg.

Get involved today! Visit
www.MorganJamesBuilds.com

Contents

Introduction

● ● ● ● ● ● ●

"Almost every successful person begins with two beliefs: The future can be better than the present. And I have the power to make it so."

—David Brooks

Your life doesn't look like you planned. You've worked hard, read the right books, talked to the right people, but you're exactly where you were a year ago. In your most honest moments, you're afraid if something doesn't change soon, you'll be in the same place again next year.

Maybe your business isn't taking off like you'd imagined. Maybe you feel like you're wasting your days at a job that isn't getting you anywhere. You have an idea or a dream, but don't know the first step to get started.

You've tried to get the success you wanted. You've asked for the raise, you've made the sales calls, you've put in the hours, but no matter what you do, you keep falling short of your goals. Sometimes you're so afraid of failing again that you stop trying altogether, and settle for just getting by.

You're tired of books, seminars, meetings, and classes that promise you success, but leave you in a perpetual place of stagnation. Maybe you're even starting to feel guilty or ashamed that you're still *here* when you dream to be *there*.

Will you *ever* get the kind of success you want?

Sure, you can probably scrape by with what you're doing now. You'll be able to pay your bills, maybe provide for your family, and if you're lucky, be able to save up enough for that new car or better house.

This isn't what you want though. You're unfulfilled, exhausted, and growing more jaded with each passing day.

I promise you that weeks will turn into months that turn into years. Before you know it, you'll be looking back at your life wondering where the time went, and more importantly when you gave up. You'll have accepted that mediocrity and mundane are your normal.

Are you willing to look back on your life and imagine what it could have been? The consequences of your inaction are irreversible. Maybe you picked up this book because you want to do something about it.

My Story

I know what it's like to struggle with these questions. I've been there. And I've helped myself and others out of this place.

By the age of 22, I was jointly managing over $160 million worth of assets. Just out of college, in a brand-new city, fresh out of an investment internship where I ranked in the top 10 percent of interns nationally, I got an incredible job at a high-level investment firm.

If only it had lasted.

After three years of working for this investment firm, I realized it was going in a different direction than I was. I could've kept working there, making a decent amount of money and been fine. But I wanted something more. One day, in the middle of a dispute with my boss, I left the company. I was ready to do it on my own. To build my business and finally get the success I wanted.

Of course, if success was easy, everyone would have it.

Moving on looked a lot different than I anticipated. During these months, there were nights I had to tell my wife, "We only have $40 to spend this week. Did you fill up your gas tank? Let's try to not use the car and eat only what we have in the cupboards."

We had to put limits on what we ate and where we could drive because we couldn't afford the gas. We had to put limits on everything we did.

You might think because I run a successful business now, that I am detached from the reality of starting from nothing and living paycheck to paycheck. I'm not. This all took place only four years ago. I'm here to tell you that this kind of situation is normal. Success must be earned. None of us have it fall into our laps.

I knew it was in my power to achieve success, and over the last four years I was able to completely build a top-level, successful financial advisement business from the ground up.

Success does take hard work and activity will get results, but the kind of rapid growth I experienced in building my business from nothing to managing 120 million dollars in just three years takes something *more*. I do not believe that success is something uncontrollable or unpredictable. I believe success is different for everyone, but that everyone can attain it.

What did I do differently?

How to Define Success

The first thing I did when I started my business was to define what success looked like for me. I have a close friend who's about ten years ahead of me in the business. When he first started out, he defined success as making a million dollars. After he made it, his goal was to make two million. He did it again. He made the two million dollars. But he still wasn't satisfied with the success he had.

"I'm not fulfilled," he told me over breakfast this morning. "I'm lost and I'm divorced. I had to sacrifice a good marriage to gain that success. I have no kids, and two of my three assistants quit on me today."

As I heard these things, I thought to myself, "If I define success by the amount of money I make, it could disappear in a day."

You need to decide what success means for you. I'm not going to tell you defining your success by a number is wrong. I'm going to tell you I won't do it. I defined what success meant for me a long time ago, and it has more to do with my family, personal growth, and my integrity than it does with how much money I make.

Google defines success[1] as "the accomplishment of an aim or purpose." Throughout the years of gaining what most might call "success," I've discovered that true success is never really finished. Instead, success is more of a journey about reaching your full potential in business, personal growth, and in your family life.

To reach your full potential is an interesting concept. You might have the most "successful" day of your life, but does that mean that tomorrow can't be better? If you make a million dollars this year, is that where you give up or do you push further, higher, and harder? Success is an everyday pursuit of getting closer to a goal and when you reach it, finally realizing you can do even more. I never thought I could write a book, but after finishing such a difficult project, I've found I can. I also know that I won't stop here.

Before you embark on the journey that this book will take you on, you first need to know where you're going. You might not end up there, but you need a planned destination, because if you don't have a plan, your boat will just sit in the harbor.

As I talk to and interview new advisors, I encourage them to stop and think of what success means for them. In business, you're often trying to play catch up. You have a sense of anxiety to make money, meet your goals, and look successful. But if you don't start by defining success, you may find yourself chasing after the wrong things. If you finally get what you worked so hard for but never actually wanted, think about how disappointed you would be.

So bookmark this page, set the book down, and take some time to think about these questions:

What do I want?
What does success mean for me?
What areas of my life do I want to have success?
What does success look like for me in business?
What kind of personal success do I want?

You should write your answers down on a separate piece of paper or in a journal. Don't read on until you have these answers, though. The worst thing for me would be if this book helped you achieve something you never really wanted in the first place.

How Do You Get There?

So, you've defined what success means for you. Great. Now that you have a destination in mind, you can start planning on how to get there.

Success is like taking a trip. For example, let's say your starting point is Los Angeles, California, but you want to get to New York City.

Having a destination is vital, but now you need a roadmap, a flight itinerary.

Benjamin Franklin said, "If you fail to plan, you are planning to fail!"

The mindsets that we will explore in the remainder of the book will serve as a steering wheel. The mindsets are described as a steering wheel because I strongly believe that you are in the driver's seat of your success. The mindsets are a tool to help guide you, but the wheel is in your hands. The wheel is made up of these seven mindsets. We will talk about everything from time management and planning for the future, to conflict and accountability.

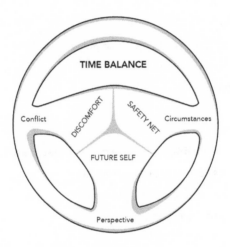

Showing you how to take hold of your success won't be the hard part. The difficult, time-consuming, and often painful price of success lies in my next question.

Will You Do It?

It's not enough to *want* success. You have to do the work to achieve it, and often the hardest work you have to do is breaking down your preconceived notions and replacing them with new ideas.

We'll revisit this again at the end of the book, but I'm convinced you shouldn't read the rest of this book if you cannot answer this question: Will you do it?

When you make plans for a trip you go through the following mental process:

1. I want to go to New York.
2. How can I get to New York?
3. I go to New York

I believe that the process for success is extremely similar, but there is one important, mental step missing from the process above.

1. I want to go to New York.
2. **Am I willing to sacrifice, work hard, and do what it takes to really get to New York?**
3. How can I get to New York?
4. I go to New York.

The mental step between our dream and our plan is the most crucial, and often overlooked part. In my opinion, not dealing with this question is the number one reason businesses fail and marriages end in divorce. We forget to ask if we're really willing to do everything it takes.

Not long ago, I worked with an advisor whom I'll call Steve. My goal was to help him be successful by pushing him. I told him to watch what I was doing. If he watched what I was doing and did the same, then he would be successful too. At the same time, I worked clients jointly with him.

His definition of success? A comfortable six figure income. His plan to get there? Follow what I was doing.

He started enthusiastically, but after a few months, I noticed some behaviors that were major hindrances to his success. He was showing up to work late on a consistent basis. He was falling asleep in the car on the way to meetings. I could also tell he wasn't studying the things I asked him to.

I showed him how he could rapidly alter and control his success, but he wouldn't make the moves himself. This junior advisor ended up leaving after six months. Not only did he fail to reach his goal, but he left frustrated, discouraged, and weary.

What if this advisor had started his journey by asking, "Am I willing to sacrifice, work hard, and do what it takes to achieve my goal?"

If he had weighed the cost beforehand and thought through what success really required of him, I am convinced he would never have started. That's okay. It really is. I wanted him to find the thing that he *did* want to pursue relentlessly, and I want the same for you.

If you are not willing to do what it takes, you are not going to reach the outcome you want.

Disclaimer: This book might not be for you if...

If you can't answer, "yes" to the question, "Will you do it?" then maybe this book isn't for you.

If you're comfortable with where you are, and don't want more, that's fine. Keep doing what you're doing, but consider putting this book down. It's not written for you.

Or maybe you *are* comfortable, but you don't *want* to be. You might be able to imagine yourself ten years from now doing the same things, but that's not where you hope to be. You want to create something more with your life than an average job and mediocre salary. If that describes you, keep reading.

I'm asking if you're willing to go the distance. I'm asking if you want more for your business, your family, and your life. Before you hop in the car bound for New York, you must decide whether you *really* want to go there. The journey is going to cost you, and the trip won't go exactly as planned. I'm asking you if it is worth it. I think it is, but now it's time for you to decide.

Maybe you picked up this book because you know it's time to start answering these questions.

If you answer yes to doing what it takes, you're ready to take on a new mindset. These mindsets will serve as your roadmap to success. For even more content and resources on these mindsets, go to www.stenmorgan.com.

In the next chapter I will explain what it is about these mindsets that will transform your life so completely. Let's get started together.

Why Mindsets?

● ● ● ⬤ ● ● ●

A few years ago, I picked up a book that claimed the secret to success hid just between it's covers. The book had a lot of great ideas and practical tools to help grow my business. By the time I finished the book, I was really fired up and excited about implementing all these success-building concepts.

A week went by, and I started trying the new techniques I learned from the book. They weren't working exactly how I had imagined, though. I grew less motivated. A month later, my life looked exactly as it had before I had picked up the success book in the first place. This is not that kind of book.

What is a Mindset?
A lot of books will help you change your actions for a short amount of time. What makes this book different is that

it's not simply about the actions you take or new habits you make.

As I built my business from $0 to over $120 million in management, I discovered success is less about the external actions and daily tasks we take in our business (the interactions with prospects and clients, the outreach, planning, and closing we do) and more about the way we approach these tasks in the process. My hope with this book is that by avoiding tips and tricks that may help you obtain *short-lived* success, it will change your perspective to help you become more successful in the long term. In other words, focusing on changing your mindsets works because the way you think holds a lasting effect on your life.

Merriam Webster Dictionary[2] defines a mindset as an established set of attitudes or beliefs held by someone. A growing body of scientific research suggests that the beliefs you have about your identity and your environment can dramatically affect your actions and your results.

There was a recent experiment[3] that exemplifies why our beliefs determine our behavior. Scientists placed a piranha on one side of a large fish tank and on the other side was a small bait fish. Between the two fish, the scientists placed a glass divider.

The hungry piranha saw the small bait fish and tried to eat it. Each time, slamming into the glass wall between them. He continued striking at the fish, but hit the glass every time. After a few hours, the piranha realized its efforts were futile and gave up.

Then the scientists removed the plexiglass partition, and both fish were able to swim freely. The piranha didn't move towards the other fish, even when the bait fish swam right in front of him. The piranha still believed he couldn't reach the other fish. The piranha grew more and more hungry, but never went near the other fish, and eventually starved to death.

What the piranha believed about his situation determined his actions. What you believe about yourself and your situation will also determine your action—or inaction.

Mindsets, in other words, are what keep us motivated, dictate our decisions, and determine our behavior.

In developing my own successful business, I have found that there are *seven* key mindsets that have shaped this journey to success. We will focus on the seven mindsets, because by changing your basic beliefs and attitudes about success, a higher quality, lasting, and meaningful level of success will follow.

It's Time to Change

I am asking you to change your mindsets. The top five most stressful life events according to *Health Status*[4] are: death of a loved one, divorce, moving, major illness, and job loss. What do those all have in common? Change.

The idea of change often evokes stress, fear, and other negative emotions. *Psychology Today* says[5], "Change is hard." Resisting change makes sense because doing what you're familiar with is much more comfortable than doing something new.

We don't normally change our circumstances or business practices because they're going well. We change because something is either *not* working or because we know that there are better opportunities beyond our current situation.

This is true not only with physical change like moving or finding a new job, but also with emotional and mental change. When something isn't going well, your first reaction might be to change your external factors like your job, your house, your team members, or even your marriage. But what if, instead, you changed the way you viewed yourself? What if you changed the limiting beliefs you have about yourself? What if you changed your belief that nothing is going to get better and started to imagine a new future? How would a new set of beliefs affect your actions? And how would a new set of actions lead to better results?

You not only *can* change the way you think and what you believe about yourself, you *need* to if you want to experience the kind of success you dreamed about in the last chapter. What you believe about yourself, your current situation, and your skillset will set the bar for your future potential. But if you resist that change, if you don't believe change is possible, for yourself and your businesses, then you'll stagnate. Not only will you not reach any new goals, the success you currently have will start to erode, leaving you further and further behind each year.

"If you want something you've never had, you must be willing to do something you've never done," said Thomas Jefferson.

In other words, if you want a new level of success, you have to *change*. The kind of change I'm talking about in this book isn't a simple change like adding a few new habits or trying the latest hot sales tactic. What I'm talking about is revolutionizing the way your brain works. I'm talking about changing the way you *think*, the way you *feel*, the way you *see* the world. It's not going to be simple or easy. You will be challenged, pushed, and asked to try things—at which you might fail.

I've never reached a new level of success by doing what got me to the previous level. There was always something new that was necessary. I am constantly learning, improving and changing my practices, and growing in these mindsets. What you need to do before you go any further is believe that you really *are* capable of greater and better things, so that you can start doing them. Without embracing change, you will never be able to use any of these mindsets. And you will be like the piranha, fooled by the belief that you *can't*.

What It *Really* Takes

In the introduction of this book, I asked you, "*Will you do what it takes?*" I told you to keep reading if you wanted to go the distance to achieve your goals. But what does it *really* take?

After building a successful financial advising firm in just three years and becoming one of the youngest advisors to achieve the Chairman's Council (the top 2-3 percent of advisors in the nation working within the same broker dealer), I've found it takes more than the textbooks teach. In school, I was taught that success was about working hard and following all the rules, and that if you did it long enough, you would see results. I don't believe in just following those long held traditional habits. You can follow them, and they may work fairly well for you, but the results I've experienced in my business could never have been achieved under that model.

The models we follow in business are influenced by how we see the world as a whole. There are two different ways people look at the world[6]. The people with the first view take the world at face value. In other words, there is little room for change. These people believe that if they are not naturally good at math, they will never be good at math. They believe if they are not creative, they never will be creative. As a result, these people believe that who they are now is who they will always be. The people with the second view see the world as a place with endless possibilities. They believe that growth is constant and that they have the power to change their skills and abilities. These people believe that who you are is always changing, improving, and growing.

The difference in these beliefs can often be seen in the way these people approach difficult problems. People with the first view approach difficult problems with dread and fear. They often are the first to give up, or say something is "too hard." The people with the second view, on the other hand, will approach difficult problems eagerly and with expectations of finding new solutions.

As a child, I viewed the world and my circumstances as something I could always improve. In the midst of chaos and uncertainty, I searched for what I could change for the better. When I used this view in business, the results were better than anything I had experienced. I knew I was on to something.

As I started my own firm, I discovered not everyone sees the world in this way. Steve, whom we talked about in the introduction, thought that because his mother was a successful advisor, it would come naturally to him too. But as he went through training and began attempting to get his first clients, he struggled. When it didn't come naturally to him as he expected, he started to grow discouraged.

He told me, "I will never be where you are." Steve had a limited belief in his potential. He refused to believe he could grow as a person, and therefore, he would never have a chance to experience Rapid, Top Level Success.

Steve didn't realize success is not about doing the least work while gaining the maximum payoff. It's about reaching your full potential.

Full potential is the development of the possible into the actual.

To achieve Rapid, Top-Level Success, you need to believe where you are now is simply a starting point and that you **are capable of far greater things**. What it *really* takes to be successful is the desire to get better every day.

As we dive into these seven mindsets, I ask that you approach each one with this in mind: New concepts and ideas can often be discouraging, but when we approach each mindset as an opportunity for growth and betterment, we find the strength and motivation to dive in.

When Can You Change a Mindset?

While it's true I first adopted new mindsets while I was growing up, that's actually not the case for most people. My mindsets changed, for the most part, because they *had* to. When I was younger and wanted to play on the school basketball team, I had to work to be able to buy the equipment I needed. I learned that if I wanted something, I had to work hard to get it. This played into how I viewed becoming successful. But just because you don't develop these mindsets in your youth, doesn't mean you won't be successful.

You might believe that to be successful you need a master's degree or a large client list or ten years experience or a lot of money in savings. You might even think you need to be single, so you have uninterrupted time to develop yourself and grow your business.

Sure, having a master's degree and an existing client list is helpful, but they aren't necessary. Too often people allow themselves to use the situations they find themselves in as excuses to avoid change.

You can't let your situation stop you from going after what you want. There will always be reasons to put off making a change. *Next year the kids will be in school. I need to wait until after I buy that car or take that trip.*

Whether you're in your twenties, fresh out of school, or in your forties and contemplating switching careers, you can make a change. Your lack of experience, or lack of contacts is not what will limit your success.

Don't let your current situation shape your future. If you're not careful, you'll find yourself believing that because of your current circumstances it's too late for you.

Here's the question you need to be asking yourself instead:

What do you need to start a fire?

I walked around my office and asked some of my teammates this question. The first person answered, "A spark." Others said similar things, "matches, kindling, and wood." A few said things like "a blowtorch or a Duraflame log."

There are a lot of ways to start a fire. Any of those answers are partially right. But what absolute, essential, bare-minimum thing you need to start a fire?

Wood.

Would it be helpful to have matches? Yes. Would a spark and kindling make starting a fire easier? Absolutely. A blowtorch and duraflame? Definitely faster. But you can also take two sticks and start a fire with friction. You work with what you have.

The same is true for changing your mindsets and becoming successful. Realistically, there are an infinite number of different ways to create success in your life. But what is the essential, bare-minimum resource? Belief and determination.

In the previous section, we talked about the belief that you are capable of far greater things. While that belief is necessary, belief without action is worthless. You can believe you can start a fire, but that won't allow you to actually start the fire. But you cannot start the fire unless you believe you can. The belief combined with determination is essential. Using both together will allow you to accomplish *any* thing at *any* time.

Although some of my mindsets were formed and changed when I was young, about half the mindsets in this book I've learned and adopted as an adult. For example, it wasn't until I started working as a financial advisor that my view and mindset on perspective changed drastically. And it took getting married and having children to adopt the time balance mindset. We are constantly learning and growing, and if you are willing and determined to embrace these changes, you will be able to start the fire, and in turn become successful.

You can change at *any* age, in *any* situation.

How Do You See the World?

These mindsets will prepare you for Rapid, Top-Level Success by showing you what business practices you need to focus on, what you need to let go of, and how to manage it all.

Before we dive into the seven mindsets, go back and identify how you see the world. Do you see yourself like Steve, who never believed he had potential, let alone that he was capable of achieving it? Or do you want to improve yourself every day—improve your mindsets, your skills, your habits as you work toward success?

How you see yourself will directly affect your success. If you see yourself as someone who can't succeed, you won't. You need to begin to believe you can grow your business into exactly what you want it to become. Only after that will embracing and implementing these mindsets be possible.

Take a moment to visualize yourself in five years. First, visualize yourself if you stayed exactly where you are now, and continued doing the same things that you've always done.

Now visualize where you would be if you adopted the view that you can be constantly changing and growing. How different would these two people be? How much does the decision you make today impact your future?

Now that we have established what mindsets are and why we are using them, it's important that we recognize where we go from here. There is a gap between where we are now and where we want to be, but how do we reveal the gap and determine the next steps? In the next chapter, we'll talk about our future selves and the two questions we need to ask ourselves.

Mindset 1
Future Self

To simply want success is not going to help you achieve it. You need to stop and imagine who you want to be personally and professionally in five years. Then, you need to figure out how to get there.

● ● ● ● ● ● ●

The Future Self Mindset is the secret to getting refocused, to figuring out what you need to be doing *right now* to achieve your goals, and to get the motivation to actually go *do it*.

You've tried to increase your sales. You're doing what you're supposed to be doing. But you keep asking yourself, "Why am I not experiencing the results?"

You might even be growing tired of the whole mundane process: the tasks, phone calls, and emails you have to send to make even one sale. It's easy to feel aimless in the midst of your daily to-do list.

Eventually, you'll feel tempted to stop doing those meaningless tasks, and you'll lose sight of where you were headed. You'll start waking up wondering why you go to work each day. I've been in this business long enough that I've watched this happen again and again.

I want it to stop happening. Over the last few years I've discovered a way to re-focus yourself and get motivated again. That's what Future Self is all about.

The Marshmallow Experiment

In the late 60's and early 70's, an experiment was done to test the concept of delayed gratification[7]. The results of the experiment are an example of how the Future Self Mindset will set you up for success.

In the experiment, children were given a marshmallow and told they could either eat the marshmallow right then, or wait for a few minutes and get a second marshmallow.

It was a simple question: Would the kids prioritize momentary pleasure, or would they hold out for the chance to double the fun. Unsurprisingly, most of the kids tried to wait—two marshmallows are better than one, after all—but only a fraction could hold out long enough to get their second marshmallow.

Interestingly, there was a direct correlation between waiting for a future reward and success later in life. The children who waited had higher SAT scores and were "significantly more competent" than the ones who couldn't wait.

On the other hand, the kids who couldn't wait had lower grades and experienced more difficulty in school and in relationships. They had a harder time saying no to peer pressure and lacked self-control.

What's going on here? And what, on earth, does a marshmallow have to do with Rapid, Top Level Success.

The first group of kids, the ones who only got one marshmallow, weren't intrinsically bad kids. Like most people, they wanted what they wanted right now, not later. We can all relate to that feeling of wanting something, even if it might not be good for us long term.

What I find amazing is *not* that the first group of kids who only got one marshmallow couldn't wait. What's interesting about this experiment, especially for our purposes, is what it shows about the power of the future self for success.

How to Get a Second Marshmallow

If you've ever watched a child waiting to eat the dessert sitting right in front of them, you can imagine the scene from this experiment. The kids with the marshmallow in front of them, desperately trying to wait, passed the time by poking their marshmallow, smelling it, or even licking it. To distract themselves, some turned their chairs around so they wouldn't have to look at the marshmallow. Others paced around the room.

But the most successful talked to themselves. They reminded themselves why they were waiting and how great it would be to have *two* marshmallows instead of just one. For some reason, when the children actively imagined the future, one in which they got the object of their desire, they were much more successful. Waiting for that marshmallow took *effort*, but that effort was made easier if the participants thought about the future.

The kids who waited weren't better people: they were employing the Future Self Mindset. They were imagining the future and reminding themselves of the payoff in waiting.

The creator of this experiment, Walter Mischel, almost fifty years after the experiments commented[8], "It's really not about candy. The studies are about achievement situations and what influences a child to reach his or her choice."

What prompts the children to choose to wait for the second marshmallow? They know their future self will be happier with two marshmallows. Later in life, what prompted these kids to do better on their SAT's? They probably knew their future self would be a lot happier if they studied and took the *effort* to succeed.

This isn't just about marshmallows anymore.

The Three Questions

Close your eyes and imagine this with me. You're at your favorite, local coffee shop and someone walks through the door and sits across from you. You look at them intently and realize that they are *you*. Maybe with a few more grays or wrinkles, they are slightly older, but still you. You begin to ask them about the future, where they are, what they're doing, maybe how much they're making—and every single answer is perfect. They are doing exactly what you want to be doing in five years. They look at you, smile, and say, "What you do now determines whether I will exist."

Your future self is who you want to be in five, ten, and twenty years. We're going through this mindset first because knowing what you want your life to actually look like is the first step to achieving it. Future Self is a tool that helps you identify what you want and what steps to take to achieve it.

When you imagine your future self, ask three questions:

1. What am I doing well?

"What am I doing well? What am I doing *now* that is bringing me closer to my goal?"

Evaluate your last few months of work, and pick out the things you are doing that are bringing you closer to your goals. Allow yourself to acknowledge your strengths so you can focus more deeply on them.

When I asked myself this question, I found that there were a lot of things I was doing really well that I wasn't giving enough time to.

2. What could I be doing better?

Ask your future self, "What could I be doing better that would help me grow faster?"

The benefit of asking this question is that you are able to cut out the distractions that are keeping you from achieving your goals, the tasks that might be draining your creativity, or the things you are doing out of obligation but not strategy.

Go so far as to ask, "Will you be proud of me in this moment?"

In fifty years when I look back on my life, I want to know that I worked as hard as I could have and didn't miss out on opportunities for growth. Asking this question helps me do that.

This can be a hard question to ask. You are probably doing things right now that are taking you *further* from your future self rather than closer. Be brutally honest with yourself. The payoff is worth it.

3. What should I do next?

The Future Self Mindset shows us where we are now and where we want to be. It reveals a large gap that can seem daunting, but allows us to create a plan.

Future Self Timeline

The Future Self Mindset helps us answer the question, **"What should I do next?"**

For me, this looked like being able to take tests and get certifications. I was able to make decisions that build upon each other by evaluating what next steps were needed in my process. The plan looks different for everyone, but it is important to determine what comes next.

Look at the diagram on the previous page. Take a minute to create your own Future Self Plan. Draw a line on a blank piece of paper. On the left side write your name and present year. This is your current self. On the far right side, put your name and the year you are imagining your future self. This could be five, ten, or twenty years in the future. Now evaluate the steps that will get you closer to the other side.

I'm not saying that you can plan the future, but you can be smart about the next steps you take towards achieving your future self, while realizing not everything goes according to plan.

Your Future Self

Each person's future self will be different because each of us are aiming for different dreams. There are moments that help you shape your future self. One big moment for me happened when I was very young.

When I was three years old, my family was living in Arizona and my mom had just married my stepdad. One night I remember hearing my mom and stepdad fighting in the room next to me. The door was closed and despite my countless efforts, I couldn't open it. The shouting from the other side was getting louder and louder. At three years old, I didn't really know what was happening, but I remember crying and relentlessly pounding on the door.

The image of me pounding on the door and not being able to help my mom is forever seared into my memory. I felt powerless in that moment and it's something I remember often.

Overcoming that feeling of powerlessness was a huge part of what shaped my future self.

I made the decision that I never wanted to be in a situation where I felt that powerless and unable to help someone I cared about. It is important for me that my future self always be able to take care of and help the people I love. That's part of why today my future self-values security, success, and helping others.

There are smaller moments, too, that define your future self. I didn't always know I wanted to be a financial advisor, but when I was a junior in college, I came one step closer to realizing what I wanted to be. I was sitting in finance class, listening to a guest speaker, a Certified Financial Analyst. He explained how he analyzed patterns in stocks and developed plans for investments and retirements. After hearing him speak, I ruled out his job, not wanting to sit behind a computer all day. But I *did* know I wanted to help people with their finances. I loved helping people and I was good with money and numbers. That's when I realized that what I was thinking about *did* have a name. It was a financial advisor. So, right there in finance class, my life completely changed course.

But just because I knew what I wanted to do, didn't mean I was using the mindset effectively. Knowing what you want to be when you grow up is not the same as using the Future Self Mindset.

It's what I asked next that made the difference. Alone in my dorm room, I imagined myself five years from that moment. I was a successful CFP. I was wearing a suit and tie, working at a top firm, making more money than anyone in my family ever had before.

"What do I need to do to get to where you are at?" I asked my future self. "What can I do right now that will get me to where I want to go?"

At that point I had no example. I had no mentor.

Honestly, I didn't have a good answer to that question. At twenty years old, I had no idea what it took to become a financial planner. But I knew just wanting to be a CFP wouldn't get me there. I began to do research, and I found that every financial advisor had to pass a set of certification tests. Most people took these tests once they had gotten a job at an investment firm, who basically pays them to take the tests for six months. My future self-wanted something faster, though. I guessed that I would be much more likely to get a good job if I already had passed the tests.

So, in my senior year of college, I decided I was going to do something different, something against the grain, something that wasn't very comfortable, but which would help me reach my future self much faster: I started studying for my certification tests. After I identified who I wanted to be, I had a clearer idea of what steps I could take so that I could start moving closer to becoming that person.

This Mindset Will Change Your Life

Your future self is not only who you want to be professionally, but personally as well. I use this exercise with my family and have seen others use it in different sports and hobbies as well. When I started to picture my future self as a father, I saw myself taking more intentional steps to become that person. My friends who use this to improve their sports performance tell me the same thing. They identify where they want to be and what they need to do to get there.

To imagine your future self is a basic reflection exercise. It is the practice of stopping to evaluate what happened and how to do it better next time. When you picture where you want to be, you are better equipped to become that person.

Each of us have different views of success, and therefore, need to tailor our future self to those views. You might define your success by how much money you make. Or what your relationship with your spouse, your children, or your friends looks like.

To develop your own view of your future self, start by going back to your definition of success, (each persons will be different) and then answer the following questions.

- What do you want your work life to look like in five years? (I.e. How much do you earn? How many hours do you work? What does your team look like?)
- What do your relationships look like? Your relationships with your family? With your friends?
- Where do you want to grow? What habits do you want to develop? What does your diet look like? What do your fitness habits look like?
- What do you want to have experienced in five years? Where will you have travelled? What did you do for fun? What did you do to expand your understanding of the world?

Often when we feel stuck or overwhelmed, it is because we lack a "future self." A mindset shift occurs when we have a picture of a goal we are working towards. We are motivated to take the next step and the meaningless tasks are given purpose and meaning.

Researchers recently studied[9] the very idea of the "future self." Their initial question: **Do we see our older selves as strangers and therefore miss out on opportunities that could later benefit us**?

Their experiment: Use digitally altered photos of a person to make them appear older to improve judgment.

These researchers put virtual reality goggles on the participants and led them into a room where they saw a virtual avatar of themselves in a virtual mirror. Half of the participants saw an avatar of their current selves, while the other half saw an avatar of themselves aged around 70.

While looking at their avatar, they were asked a series of personal questions like, "What is your name? Where are you from? What are your passions?"

The interaction lasted between 60-75 seconds.

After this, participants were asked to imagine they had received $1,000 and asked them to allocate it into four different places: use it to buy something nice for someone special, invest it in a retirement fund, plan a fun and extravagant occasion, and put it into a checking account.

The participants who were exposed to their future selves in virtual reality allocated more than twice as much money to the retirement account than those who just saw their current selves.

Co-researched Laura Carstensen commented, "It's fascinating. It really did have an effect. When people can really connect to themselves and say, 'That person at age 70, that's me, actually,' they tend to want to take care of that person more."

Using this mindset is a way to consider the repercussions of your actions without the risk of wasting time doing things that won't really help you obtain your goal. Essentially, you have more power to manage your potential future regrets.

To use this mindset, the first thing you have to do is stop and ask yourself, "In five years will I look back on this and think it was worthwhile?"

Intentionality

The Future Self Mindset enables you to make more focused and intentional decisions. Intentionality is key in achieving success, because success rarely happens by chance. Instead, it happens when we intentionally work towards it and make decisions that reflect our future self.

Each decision you make can be filtered through your future self. When faced with a decision you need to ask, "**Will this bring me closer to my future self?**" If not, you have the ability to say no and make the decision with clarity.

For example, one of the hardest things every salesperson has to do is make sales calls. I watch the other advisors in my office *dreading* the idea of making sales calls. When using future self, it is easier to decide to not only do the calls, but realize that they can actually be a way to make new clients and help more people. You also realize that sales calls aren't all your future self wants to do. Maybe you want to start public speaking, and teaching seminars as a way to tell more people about your business. You may have dreaded this idea before you imagined your future self, but looking at their success gives you confidence that you can achieve more than you thought possible.

Intentional decision making applies not only to big decisions, but daily tasks as well. When we filter our daily to-do lists through our future self, we can eliminate more tasks that don't bring us closer to our goal. This way we are saving more time and resources to focus on what works.

Fire Yourself

If you enter the Future Self Mindset deeply enough, eventually, you will reach that point when the goals your future self was working toward aren't big enough anymore. You will have achieved so much progress toward your potential that you will realize there is a whole new level of potential you can unlock. At this point, you will have to fire your future self and begin setting new goals and challenge yourself even further.

It is a great accomplishment to hit goals and make big deals, but I've seen too many salespeople give up after doing that. They take a few weeks off, go on vacation, and stop trying because they achieved what they wanted to. There is a time and place to celebrate accomplishments, but you need to realize that your outward achievements are not your end goals.

Early in my business, I did this exercise and imagined my future self five years down the road. I decided that in my business I wanted to be a leader of a team, achieved the Chairman's Council (the top two-three percent of advisors in the nation with my broker dealer), and have a healthy, successful business with a high customer retention rate.

In 2015, I looked back at the person I had decided my future self was going to be and realized that I had become that person. It was amazing to see all the hard work pay off. I celebrated with my wife and then immediately thought to myself, "What next?"

Your future self allows you to start working towards a legacy. Now you can ask yourself the question, "What legacy do I want to leave?"

When you reach your future self and become the person you worked so hard to be, you need to stop again and reflect. You need to "fire your old future self," so that you can develop even more potential and achieve even more success.

Future Self in Action:

If you haven't already, stop and define five traits that make up your future self. Now choose the top two of those traits. Write them down, and under each one, identify three "steps" you can take to get closer to that trait or goal. You now have an idea of *who* you want to be and *how* to get there.

Now that we know where we're going and are able to identify things that will bring us closer to our goals, we need to recognize the things we think are keeping us safe, but are in reality holding us back. We can succeed greater and higher than we know, we just need to push ourselves to the point where we have no other choice. In the next chapter, we'll explore removing our safety nets so that we can unlock more of our full potential.

Mindset 2
Remove Your Safety Net

The fastest way to success is through risk so high that achieving your goal becomes your only option and failure would result in total loss.

● ● ● ● ● ● ●

Everything you want is on the other side of fear.
—Jack Canfield

There are a lot of good things in your life that keep you safe. When you were young, your parents kept you safe by providing for your physical needs. Your house keeps you safe from rain and cold. Your job keeps you safe from poverty and starvation.

However, some of these do more than keep you safe. They can also hold you back.

Success is always achieved through risk, and Rapid, Top Level Success is achieved through even *more* risk.

This is how you accomplish more than you ever imagined: you let go of everything that has been holding you back.

How can you realize your true potential unless you've abandoned your safety nets? Often, you don't realize what's holding you back until it's too late.

Steve and Tim

When I first hired Steve, he seemed eager, and I was excited to see him reach his full potential.

I began training him. I took him with me when I met with clients or spoke at events. I even consulted on clients jointly with him to get him started.

Slowly, I got the feeling Steve wasn't enjoying the work we were doing. His interests peaked whenever the idea of success or money was brought up, but he consistently came into work late and wasn't putting in the effort required to be successful in this business. Week after week, I could tell he was staying up late, and when he did make it to work on time, he had clearly rushed out of bed.

A few months into the job I asked Steve to come to my office. "Do you really want this?" I asked him.

He shrugged his shoulders and replied, "I guess."

Advisors are paid on commission and I was concerned he wasn't making enough money to live. So I asked him, "If you're not making enough sales, how do you pay your bills?"

He answered slowly, "My parents…"

And suddenly, it all made sense.

Steve didn't care because he didn't have to care. He had no urgency, no real need to be successful, so why would he break a sweat trying? He had no family to support, no wife, no children, no mortgage payments, no student loans. Nothing was pushing him.

You Need Urgency

Around the same time, I had another advisor join my team. Let's call him Tim. Tim had been a professional football player in the NFL for several years. He received a monthly pension that was enough to pay his bills and live comfortably.

When he began working with the team, I could immediately tell he didn't have the same level of investment as I did. I pushed him, knowing that he could achieve so much more than he was settling for.

At first Tim was interested in what achieving more would look like. However, after a week or two, he decided he didn't want to do all the hard work. With his pension coming in, he explained, he was comfortable where he was. He just wanted a little extra cash, and the flexibility of the job.

For Tim and Steve, there was no urgency, and there wasn't any desire for more success or growth. They weren't motivated to do the work it would take to be successful, and they didn't see the need to put in the kind of work that success requires.

Tim never saw the value in his work, and couldn't seem to get himself motivated. He was doing some of the things I told him to be successful. He wasn't experiencing results, though, because he didn't have the right mindset. And he wasn't going to experience better results, certainly not Rapid, Top-Level Success, unless he changed his thinking.

What is a Safety Net?

A safety net is something that provides a margin of security or protection. We think we need them to keep us safe when in reality they are the very things holding us back. For Steve, it was the money he received from his parents. For Tim, it was the pension from the NFL. When I first got out of college my safety net was my comfortable job at an investment firm.

In 2011, I ventured to start my own practice and in doing so, removed my safety net. At that point, I was an Oregon boy living in Nashville with no clients, very few connections, and very little savings left. This was the biggest challenge of my life thus far. I would find myself putting on my suit and driving to my office with no idea what to do next. The only thing I did know for sure was that failure was not an option. I did not have any family to help me financially and I was no longer part of a successful firm. There was no safety net.

Although I left the company suddenly and had no idea what to expect, it was the best thing that I could have done. It was extremely stressful, but I needed that push to get me moving. I knew how much I had to lose if I actually failed, and that made me work that much harder.

The Bravest Thing You've Ever Done

Maybe you've thought of pursuing your dream of success, hesitantly working at it in your spare time while you stare out your office window. The problem is you've never really gone all in, fully committing yourself to your idea and the pursuit of success.

It is our safety nets that are holding us back.

Fear is what is keeping most of you from removing the safety net. We are afraid of failing, afraid of looking stupid, and afraid we won't be able to provide for ourselves or our families.

Not only is fear keeping you from making the decision, but it might be the only motivator you have to make the decision as well.

I want you to close your eyes and imagine this with me:

You're 75 years old. Some days your bones ache, and your body fights you. You and your spouse are retired, and live a comfortable life somewhere warm.

It's Christmas time and you're sitting in your rocking chair as you await the rest of the family to arrive. The door flings open as your kids and their families rush in. Your grandchildren fill the room and fight over sitting on your lap. One of them looks up while sitting on your lap and asks, "Tell us a story. What's the bravest thing you've ever done?"

You look down at them and open your mouth.

Are you going to tell them the story of stepping out and risking everything to follow your dream and pursue success? Or will you change the subject and tell someone else's story of bravery?

What you choose to do now is what will determine what you tell your grandchildren.

You have two options: stay in the same situation and continue to receive the same results or choose to pursue true success.

My Safety Net

I was a freshman in high school when the man that I called Dad, who had raised me for 11 years, walked out on my family. He left my mom with four children and very few resources. She hadn't worked for over 20 years, and now she had to find a job to support us.

My mom didn't choose for her safety net to be removed, nor do I want this to happen to anyone else, but it was only through this situation that she was forced to grow in a way she had previously never imagined and I discovered the idea of safety net and what it meant for success.

To support the family, my mother started a drive-through coffee kiosk. They were popular in Oregon at the time, and the startup costs weren't too high. Looking back now, I realize that failure was not an option for her. She had no safety net. She had to find a way to make it work, or her and her children wouldn't have a place to sleep or food to eat. She worked hard and found us a house, and made sure we all had everything we needed. But getting to that point required a tenacity I'd never seen in her before.

In this situation, my mom could have chosen to be a victim, or give up, but she chose to pursue what was uncomfortable and hard for the people she loved. When I saw my mom respond in that way, it shaped how I responded to hard situations. I thought, "Oh, so that's what you do. You don't give up, there's no choice. You push through it."

We all have a story that has shaped the person we are today. Some of us have faced very difficult journeys, while others may be able to say that we have not faced much hardship in our lives.

No matter the journey, we all need to recognize our mental and even physical safety nets that hold us back.

Human Needs

As humans, we have needs to live and live well. The diagram below is Maslow's Hierarchy of Human Needs[10]. The most important needs (bottom level) are the physiological needs. These are our most basic needs such as food, water, and shelter. The second most important needs are those of safety, which include: personal security, job security, health insurance, and safe living environment. Maslow believed that before a person could reach the next level in the pyramid, they would need to have attained the level below it.

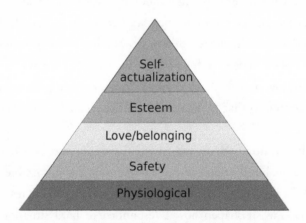

Maslow contended that these needs actually dominated one's actions and until we reached these next steps, we would be perpetually stuck.

Why remove your safety net if it's actually a basic need?

Removing your safety net is not about your assets, income, house, or your parent's money. Getting rid of your safety net is about taking responsibility. It's time you become your own safety net. You need your action and your ability to take action to become your safety net.

Like Steve, whose parents would send him a check whenever he needed, but that money and security wasn't his. Or Tim—he had earned that monthly check, but it was holding him back from pursuing more.

What safety net are you relying on? Family? An average job that simply pays the bills? Your own low expectations of yourself?

Remove the Safety Net

I have a friend who always dreamed of being a writer. He graduated with a bachelor's degree in English. After graduation, he kept the idea in the back of his mind and instead of pursuing his dream he began to settle for other jobs. He felt pressure to have a "real job" and earn a steady paycheck. It wasn't until 2011 that he decided to make his dream happen. He left his job and spent all his time writing and honing his skills until he actually became a full-time writer. Now, four years later, he has a successful company that helps other aspiring writers make their dreams of becoming writers come true. By removing his safety net, he was able to pursue his dream.

If you spend your nights tossing and turning as you secretly imagine what it might be like to be *really* successful, you're just going to grow weary.

The first step in choosing to pursue your career, business, or dream is removing your safety net. Removing your safety net means first, determining what it is that might be holding you back or keeping you comfortably "safe," and then removing it from your life.

Imagine you're twenty-two, and fresh out of college. You dream of starting your own business in the city. So you move to a new city, find an apartment, and begin working. You have no family or friends that will let you sleep on their couch if all fails. You really only have two options: succeed or die trying. It is often in these places, when we have no other option than to make it work, we succeed. No great success was ever achieved without the risk of losing everything.

I'm not telling you to go out today, leave your job, and sell your house. I'm saying *today,* you need to imagine yourself with no safety net and decide what in your life is holding you back. The time is now, whether you're older and not sure what the next steps are or fresh out of college.

The consequences of not removing your safety net are mediocrity and dissatisfaction. The longer you wait to remove your safety net, the harder it becomes. The longer you wait the more responsibilities you may have to a spouse and children and taking necessary risks will be more difficult. You have the luxury of choosing whether you will remove your safety net. But you have to make the decision. Putting yourself in that position will make you more likely to succeed.

●　●　●　●　●

I am reminded of a scene from a Batman movie. Christian Bale, Batman, is stuck in a prison. The prison has no guards, and no bars. The only way out is to climb a massive stone pit, grabbing the bricks that bulge from the interior.

Bale practices the escape time and time again. He fastens a rope to his waist as he practices his escape. We watch as he climbs and reaches for one of the bricks. It crumbles beneath his fingers and he falls and is left dangling from the rope.

A blind prisoner asks him, "How can you move faster than possible? Fight longer than possible? If not from the most powerful impulse of the spirit—the fear of death, the will to survive."

"I don't fear death. I fear dying in here while my city burns with no one there to save it."

"Then make the climb."

"How?"

"As the child did. Without the rope. Then fear will find you again."

Bale packs his belongings, throws the sack on his back and approaches the wall. The prisoners begin to gather and a man extends the rope to him. He denies the rope, and reaches for the brick wall.

The prisoners gather and begin chanting. They all know if he falls now, he's dead. He has no rope, no safety net waiting for him. It's do or die.

Half way up is a platform that many have reached in the past. The only thing standing between him and the escape is the leap to another platform. He's fallen time and time again but was caught by the rope around his waist.

Now failure is not an option. Nothing will catch him if he falls.

He looks towards the platform in front of him and then back to his feet and moves them closer to the edge. A small piece of rock falls from the platform he's standing on. He closes his eyes and breathes in deep. He exhales, leaps to the platform, and grabs the edge of the pit. He pulls himself up, in disbelief and utter shock. He did it.

It took removing the mental and literal safety net to make the leap and escape. When failure is not an option, we are more likely to succeed.

Maybe getting out of your pit requires letting go of the rope that's keeping you tied there. On the other side of the pit are your dreams and potential success. It could be the business you want to build or the house you want to buy for your family. Whatever it is, there's a difficult journey you have to take, and a wall you might have to climb. You need to identify what is holding you back and let it go.

Stress Helps You

Removing your safety net will most definitely cause you some sort of stress, but stress is actually one of the secrets to Rapid, Top-Level Success. You might think, "Stress? How can more stress help me achieve success?"

Stress is a powerful emotion. I've seen people's lives completely destroyed by stress, but I have also seen people's lives dramatically changed for the better thanks to stress.

Stress is simply our body's reaction to outward circumstances[11]. Contrary to popular belief, stress can be a *good* thing, especially when it comes to motivating and creating urgency in our lives. There is a healthy amount of stress that will push us to do the things we need to do to be successful.

Stress is useful until a certain point, until it becomes debilitating.

A study from the *Harvard Business Review*[12] asked participants to look at stress inducing images, while in a brain scan. When they were asked to label the emotion, the study revealed that the stress actually gave participants a more heightened awareness, and an improved response.

In other words, stress can create more positive, helpful reactions. Physically, this looks like muscles that react faster and ears that hear better. Mentally, the same happens. Our brains become more aware of the situation around us and can processes more information than normal.

The advisor I mentioned earlier, Steve, let stress cripple him. He was experiencing stress, but not allowing it to motivate him. The stress he felt only created more feelings of guilt for not going the distance.

Allow the stress of releasing our safety net to motivate us to change, and to create an urgency within us. How can we find the right level of stress that skirts right up to the max level between focus and crippling? How can we use stress to our advantage?

When aiming high for success, stress is often a positive reaction. For example, an aspiring writer needs the stress from deadlines in their life, or they'll never finish their projects. Just like an advisor needs the stress of meeting their goals.

We will often stress more over the things and people that are most important to us. Stress shows that we care and place value in something. This is where the motivation comes from.

As I mentioned previously, stress also can give us a sense of urgency. The other advisor I mentioned previously, Tim, never experienced this sense of urgency. With the checks from his pension, there was never a desperate pressure to succeed.

If Tim had taken his pension checks and put them all in savings, not allowing himself to use the money, he might have had a healthy amount of stress that would push him to take more responsibility for his own success.

Removing the safety net gives stress a healthy say in your life. It is important to find the balance between a healthy amount of stress and a dangerous amount of stress. Not only can too much stress be bad, but it can be harmful and produce the opposite effects of urgency and motivation. Stress has the power to motivate us or paralyze us. What stress will you allow in your life?

Why Fear?

King George VI[13] was king of Britain during World War 2. He also had a severe stammer and dreaded public speaking. When war began to break out in the late 1930's, King George knew he needed to do something about it. He knew he needed to prepare his country for the consequences of war. He had been afraid of public speaking for most of his life. Yet on September 3rd 1939, even though he was terrified of failing, the king delivered a speech that began a war, and rallied the people.

He said:

The task will be hard. There may be dark days ahead, and war can no longer be confined to the battlefield, but we can only do the right as we see the right, and reverently commit our cause to God. If one and all we keep resolutely faithful to it, ready for whatever service or sacrifice it may demand, then with God's help, we shall prevail.

It's normal to be afraid of public speaking or afraid of failure. But we can't let that stop us from pursuing and overcoming those fears.

Fear is our bodies' response to danger, both physical and emotional. Fear tells us that there is a real threat that we need to protect ourselves from.

Often though, we fear situations that aren't life or death, and we miss out on opportunities because of that fear. We've experienced pain in our past that can often trigger an irrational fear that keeps us from more experiences like developing relationships, new job opportunities, or expanding a business.

For example, a girl who grew up with abusive parents might have difficulty trusting authority figures, such as a boss, later on in life. Although the woman, as an adult, might know that she can trust authority, she will most likely always experience triggers that cause her to fear.

Fear is an important aspect of removing your safety net. Your fear is trying to tell you there is potential danger, but you need to evaluate how serious the danger is and if it's worth pressing into. With success and the things we're talking about, the fear is almost always something you need to fight.

Fear triggers a fight or flight response in your brain[14]. Your brain will release chemicals that speed up your reactions, tense your muscles, and create an overall alertness in your body.

Fear of a stranger with a gun is a real and important fear that helps us make life-preserving decisions. But when it comes to our dream and success, our fears tell us, "What if you fail?" or "What if you look stupid?" Our fear often convinces us that flight is the answer, when the truth is, if you want to be successful, you need to fight.

We would live in a different world if Bill Gates let his fear rule his decisions. What if Hemingway was too afraid to have his work published? Or if Walt Disney listened to his boss who fired him saying, Disney, "lacked imagination and had no good ideas."

The fear of never trying, never knowing, and never reaching your full potential outweighs the fear of failing.

There are people whose names you do not know and will never know because they allowed their fears to stop them. Will you join them? Or will you join the lists of people who faced their fears and lived lives full of success? Are you going to choose to act or stay paralyzed by fear?

Challenge
Imagine this with me:

You're standing on a ledge, before you is the ocean, and behind you are all your family and friends. The ocean is deep, blue, and warm. You're getting ready to jump, but you feel something tugging around your waist. Looking down, you discover a rope tied around you, the end of the rope leads behind you. You look and see the rope tied to your lifestyle, your fear of failure, your family and friends.

This rope has kept you safe, but something inside you is telling you to let it go. You know you'll be safe without it. You want to know the feeling of jumping freely, knowing you can swim further than the rope allows.

You move your hands to the knot in the rope and slowly untie it. You lay the rope on the ground next to you, and turn around to look behind you. Your family and friends are still there, and you hear them, "We know you can do it."

Removing your safety net, untying this rope, does not mean you say goodbye to everything behind you. It means you are allowing yourself to jump further, swim deeper, and reach further than you thought you could with the rope around your waist. You are giving yourself the freedom to believe in your own abilities and take responsibility to jump on your own.

I'm not telling you to go out and leave your job. I'm saying you need to know that you *could* leave your job.

You need to think about the things that are holding you back. They might be things that you think are keeping you safe, but what they're doing is keeping you comfortable, and tied to the wall of the prison.

You need to know that if all your resources were taken from you, you'd still make it. If your clients left, your website crashed, or you were fired from your job, you could still say, "I can do it." Our minds are our greatest obstacle. Whether it is the fear of the unknown or fear of failure, we all know that we are capable of doing things that we just don't do.

SAFETY NET IN ACTION:

Take a few minutes to create a list of the things in your life keeping you safe. Go through the list and ask yourself, "Could this be holding you back from pursuing the success I want?" After identifying your "safety nets," imagine what it would look like to remove those. Would removing those motivate you to achieve a higher level of success?

When we release ourselves from these safety nets, we are motivated and willing to do whatever it takes. But what is it exactly that you're going to do? How do you know the steps to take on this newfound journey? In the next chapter, we'll discuss how input from others in the business is the fastest and most effective way to reach your goals and avoid costly mistakes.

Mindset 3
Perspective

The mistakes and achievements of others are the best teachers on the path to success. Seek out and accept the perspective of mentors, peers, and customers.

● ● ● ● ● ● ●

I magine you're driving through an unfamiliar city. You're headed to an important business dinner on the other side of the city. You have a general idea of where you need to go, but your GPS isn't working and keeps telling you that your car is in the nearby creek. You take a left out of your hotel, hoping to find a road sign, but the road is under construction and closed. You turn right down a one-way street and realize you're going the wrong "one-way." Quickly, you turn onto the first street you find and see a gas station in the distance. You decide to stop for directions.

You begin to ask the man at the register who starts telling you to head east, then northwest, and then left. You nod politely, but don't have a compass, so you're feeling pretty hopeless.

Suddenly a man who has been standing nearby speaks up, "Excuse me, I overheard your dilemma. I'm actually headed that way if you want to follow me."

With no other options, you agree, get into your car, and begin following him. You're still a little unsure, but you keep close behind his car. After a minute of driving, you hit some heavy traffic, but the man takes a right down a side street and you follow him. After another minute and a few more side roads, you look behind you and realize you somehow got around all the traffic.

You're driving for a few more minutes and suddenly the car you're following slows, and so curiously, you do too. You drive a few hundred yards and see a hidden cop car pointing his radar gun at you, but since you slowed down, you were well under the speed limit.

You realize you are approaching your destination, and you follow the car as it pulls over to park. The man gets out of his car and walks up to your window and says, "You can park here if you are going to be here less than two hours. The cops patrol this street every hour. But I have a buddy around the corner who owns the pizza shop. You can park in his back lot for as long as you need."

By this point, you're sufficiently impressed by this man's generosity and knowledge of the city. "Thank you." you tell him, "You really know your way around here."

"Yeah, there are some great shortcuts to avoid traffic on the east side. And those cops are always hiding on that road back there trying to catch people speeding. Oh, and over there, he pointed behind him, "some of the best coffee this side of town."

"Perfect, I was looking for a good place online last night. Thanks again for all the help."

"No problem, I've lived in the city for twenty years now. I like showing the rookies around." He says as he waves and gets back in his car.

You walk through the door to the restaurant for your meeting and check your phone. You're ten minutes early and have multiple texts from the rest of your team saying they're stuck in traffic and will be late.

You think about how that would have been you stuck in traffic, or how you probably would have gotten pulled over by the police officer. You realize how there's no way you could have gotten here without the help from the man who knew the city so well.

This is what my first few years of business felt like. Some days I felt like I was driving through a new city without a map, wandering hopelessly towards a destination. And other days, I found guidance and seemed to avoid the traffic and get closer to my destination a lot quicker.

It's okay to not know how to get somewhere you've never been, whether you're driving or working in sales. That's normal.

There is often a pressure to feel like you need to know about everything in the business. I used to feel like that, until I realized I can't know what I don't know.

I'm not saying you'll never get to your destination if you go alone, but by asking for input, you will most likely get there faster and maybe with a few less speeding tickets.

Definition of Perspective

Perspective, as defined by Merriam Webster[15], is, "A way of portraying three dimensions on a flat, two-dimensional surface by suggesting depth or distance." In our context, perspective is the ability to see a situation or idea in a different light or from a new angle. We are able to see old things in new ways.

Perspective can be something that makes or breaks your business. Perspective is the advice your boss gives you, or the comment your customer makes. Whatever form it takes, perspective and the input of others often finds you, and when it does, you need to make the choice to listen and be open to the feedback. However, simply *accepting* others' perspectives won't lead you to Rapid, Top-Level Success. It is something you need to actually seek out.

Seeking out what I *don't* know is something I do constantly. I recently partnered with an ex-Navy Seal coach to work with my team, not for his financial firm expertise or because I thought he could improve my number of assets under management. I hired him because I needed someone who had served on one of the very best teams in the world to show me what I didn't know about team building.

In order to grow my business, I needed to ask for input from others. And so do you.

Growing Up Without Perspective

Perspective wasn't always something that has come easy to me. Growing up, I trusted very few people. I had a history of issues with authority figures and therefore rarely listened to what people would have to say. This was mostly due to the fact that I had five different father figures growing up, and with each new guy, I grew more skeptical and feelings of rejection clouded my view.

I remember one in particular didn't just leave our family, he actively tried to make it worse for us after leaving. He tried suing us, taking our house, and would not leave us alone until we were left with almost nothing. I didn't have an authority figure who was consistent enough in my life to trust.

These problems followed me throughout high school and college too. In high school, I would constantly disagree with basketball coaches and never allowed them to coach me. They would then bench me, which limited my growth on the team as well as the team's full potential. The same thing happened in college, potentially ruining my basketball career. These coaches tried to give me perspective, tried to show me that my actions were hurting me, but I wouldn't listen. I constantly believed they didn't really care or have my best interest in mind.

After college, I started at a financial firm and as every new financial advisor does, I had to make a lot of sales calls. And as any young, inexperienced financial advisor also does,

I made a few mistakes. There was one potential client who was interested and I was trying to close a deal with. I called him and told him there was new urgent information about the deal. (Rule #1. Never use the word **urgent** when leaving a message with a secretary.)

It was the third or fourth time I had called him, and saying that something was urgent, when realistically it could have waited, definitely lost me the client. Not only did he ask me to never call him again, but he also filed a complaint with the company I was working for.

A few days later I called my biological dad, who I had begun developing a better relationship with, and told him what happened with the sales call.

"What were you thinking?" My dad responded, as if I should have known better.

Surprised, angry, and frustrated with his question I yelled into the phone, "How would I know?? Why don't you teach me something!"

We were both silent for a moment before he said, "You know, you're right. I'm sorry. I should have used this opportunity to teach you."

Years of hurt and anger were confronted with that conversation. That moment was a huge breakthrough for me, even though it was out of anger and years of frustration, I asked my dad to teach me something. Not everything was fixed, but from that moment forward I was able to change my mindset on perspective.

It took confronting and forgiving my dad to realize that I was missing out on the perspective and advice from others. I stopped believing the rest of the world was trying to hurt me, and slowly began trusting and listening to authority figures.

The Johari Window

The Johari Window[16] is a psychological tool that was developed in 1955 and can be used to help you better understand your relationship with yourself and with others. The Johari Window, (pictured right) has four quadrants: what is known by everyone, what is known by just you, what is known by others, and what is unknown by both parties.

Johari Window

	Known to self	Not known to self
Known to others	Arena	Blind Spot
Not Known to Others	Façade	Unknown

Although this concept is often used in psychology, I have found it valuable to help find the path to success in business.

Take a look at the chart again. The top left quadrant is what is known by everyone in your business. These are the common business practices taught in textbooks like cold calling, following up with clients by email, and going to conferences.

The box on the bottom left is filled with things that are known by you, but not known by others. These are the competitive advantages that set your business apart from the competition. This could be the products and services you offer, or the way you treat your customers. Either way, to be successful, you need to leverage what you know.

The bottom right box is filled with the unknowns of your business, things neither you nor your peers know. This is the box that everyone is on the search to uncover. When *Blue Ocean Strategy* was published in 2005, the idea revolutionized how business was viewed. The idea was largely unknown to everyone. This is an example of the bottom right box.

The top right box is filled with the things known by others, but not known by you. We want to know the ins and outs of the business, the shortcuts, and best practices. This box is filled with things you don't know, and the only way to change that is to find the people that do know and start asking them.

You could look at me and my business and say, "Yeah, that guy is successful. He must be doing a lot of great stuff." That might be true, but if I settled for that, I wouldn't stay successful for long. It's more important for me to figure out what I'm *not* doing, to fill in the unknowns of my personal Johari window, especially those things neither I nor my competitors know.

The Johari Window reminds us that that there will always be things you don't know. That's normal and okay, but recognizing it doesn't mean you stay where you are. If you want to set yourself apart from the competition, you need to go in search of the things you don't know. I have found that the only way to uncover those things is through seeking the perspectives and expertise from three different groups of people: mentors, peers, and your customers. Each group offers different, but valuable perspective that could change your entire business.

Perspective from Mentors

As I have helped others achieve success, I have discovered that getting perspective from others is often the missing step between where you are now and where you want to be. While it might be difficult to admit it, you currently lack the knowledge to take the next steps towards your future self. What good is having a picture of who you want to be without the directions to get there?

In the 1600s, when a young person wanted to learn a trade, he submitted himself as an apprentice to a craftsman with many years of experience. For as many as ten years, the apprentice would live with his master and help him with all his projects. In return, the master craftsman would provide an education, passing down everything he knew about his craft to the apprentice.

Although apprenticeships have mostly disappeared over the last four hundred years, the basic principle is still widely helpful. There is only so much you can learn from books and courses. I would not be where I am now without the knowledge and practice I gained from working for and learning from other financial advisors when I was first getting started. No matter what you're doing, it's the same for you.

It can be hard to find a "master" willing to teach you everything you need to be successful in your business. What I am sure you *can* find, though, is a role model, someone who has the success you want. For me, I searched out people who were in positions I wanted to be in five years from then, both personally and professionally. Once I found them, I would ask how they got where they were and what advice they could give someone who wanted what they had.

This is what you need to do. You need to recognize that you can't do it alone. You can't teach yourself everything, and when you try, you end up tired and frustrated. In my experience, I'm often surprised by the amount of help and advice I'm given. Most people are more than willing to offer advice on how to get where they are. Finding someone who has been where you are and has learned better ways to get there isn't as hard as it seems.

Step one: Identify the success you are working towards. (Look back at Future Self.)

Step two: Find five people that have that success and ask to meet with them. (E-mail them, send them a letter, call their office, etc.)

Step three: Ask these people three questions: What business practices best helped you reach your goal? What do you wish you had done more of in the last five years? If you could do it over what would you change?

Step four: Take their advice and see how it fits into your life and business, then implement what might work for you.

Step five: Use their advice for six months and let the person know how it worked. If it worked well, thank them and ask if they have further advice from there. If it didn't work well, ask them if there's something you are missing or can potentially change.

What I have learned from listening to different mentors over the last few years is to take the best practices from each person. I ask each mentor, *"What is working best for you?"* I take that information and change it to work with my business. When I do that, I end up having the best business practices of the most successful people I know.

Perspective from Peers

An often unexpected, but valuable source of new perspective comes from our peers and team members.

I was recently told a story by a retired navy seal who worked for many years in the Middle East.

The Navy Seals needed to extract a group of civilians from the shore of a river, but they didn't have a big enough boat.

The team threw around different ideas, but none were viable. They couldn't figure out what to do. At the back of the room, there was a young soldier who wasn't part of the Seal team and had a much lower rank.

During a short silence, he spoke up, "I saw that a prince lives down the road," he said, although he probably shouldn't have been speaking, "who had a yacht that might be big enough to get the job done."

It was the first solid piece of input they had, and even though it came from someone who didn't have the most authority, the team ended up borrowing the yacht, rescuing the civilians, and completing their mission.

I've learned to do this is my own business. I have a lot of team members who have been financial advisors for years, and then I have one member of my team who is fairly new to the business. In group meetings, it is often Dan, the new advisor, who has fresh, new ideas that others don't because he hasn't had his head down doing this business for thirty years.

Peers and team members are often the ones who know you and your business practices best. They can offer advice you haven't thought of, or recognize areas you can improve in.

These people also aren't limited to your field of expertise. It is actually better to get advice and perspective from people in *different* fields because you are exposed to new, different, and sometimes better ideas to grow your business. Each time I meet with someone I ask what is working for them in their business, what advice they have for me, and how I can help them and their clients meet their goals.

Our peers almost always specialize in something different than us. A friend of mine who used to be a project manager for a company that made jet engines for commercial airlines described their process of designing and testing their engines to me once. Every engine has thousands of pieces and hundreds of things that could go wrong. (Similar to running a successful business.) No one person could successfully build a great jet engine. My friend told me that since there were so many intricate parts, his team was made up of people who specialized in many different areas. For example, there were Turbine Fan Blade Specialists, whose only job was to develop and work with the edges of fan blades in the engine, as well as, test cell mechanics, general mechanics, drafters, and metrics specialists.

"In order to be successful, I needed the others on my team. Yes, I studied engineering and had quite a bit of experience in developing engines, but there's no way I could know everything. I could have probably designed an engine by myself, but it wouldn't have been as good. "When you take the best from everyone around you, you'll end up with the best product. That's what made my team so successful."

They were successful. Their engine is in the new Airbus 350a, one of the fastest, most fuel-efficient airplanes in the world.

I asked him, "So after designing and building multi-million-dollar jet engines, everything else must seem easy."

"Actually," he responded, "No. Each new problem has a new set of challenges. Just because I can build jet engines doesn't mean I can sell life insurance. The unknowns are different in every project. It might seem easy after this, but there are always things I need to learn."

He emphasized, "I needed *each* of those people to be successful."

It's not realistic to think that we can know everything about every business. At most, each of us have a few areas of expertise and a basic understanding of most other areas. When I need someone who has an expert understanding of insurance sales, I'll ask the member of my team who specializes in that. If I need legal advice, I'm going to ask a lawyer. The same situation occurs when you go to the doctor.

You don't see your primary care physician if you want your eyes checked.

No matter what profession you are in, the perspective and expertise of others is one of the most valuable tools to grow that you can have.

The Best Source of Perspective is Your Customers

By changing your perspective, you are able to see new things. And often the things you see will change your actions.

An example of this is what happens when you drive a car. When you switch lanes, you check your mirrors before moving. But unfortunately, mirrors don't show the whole picture. There are still blind spots in your line of vision. By looking beside you, you can see cars that weren't in your mirror. If you do see a car beside you, you won't switch lanes.

To be successful, you need to be able to see situations in a different light. A few years ago, I lost a client to a competitor because they had a different perspective.

The other advisor had listened more carefully to the client and remembered them saying they wanted all their documents packaged together in a way they could pass on to their kids in case anything happened. He listened, and created a binder with all the client's documents and information. Afterward, my clients switched their business to the other advisor.

All I could think was, "A binder? Seriously? If they needed anything they could always ask me. Why would they switch advisors over a binder?" At first, I was confused and frustrated, but then I realized it had nothing to do with a binder.

From my perspective, I knew their kids and if anything happened, their kids would come to me. But from their perspective, the binder brought a level of security and peace of mind they felt they needed.

In sales, you need to recognize that there are more perspectives than your own. If you don't recognize these perspectives, you are in danger of losing business.

When I realized that the perspective my customers had was more important than what I thought, success quickly followed. My biggest sales came when I worked hard to figure out the perspective my would-be clients had, *not* when I focused on imposing my own perspective on others.

You've heard it a million times: *the customer is always right.* But I've learned to think of it a little differently. Although I may know financial products better, I have to put my perspective aside and listen to the customer's. The customer may or may not be right, but the customer's *perspective* is always more important.

Are there mentors, peers, or customers that you need to be listening to?

Perspective in Action:
We identified three different kinds of people you can get perspective from: your peers, mentors, and clients. Identify a specific peer, mentor, and client that you can get perspective from, and ask them to meet. As you meet with them, be prepared to ask hard questions about how you can be even better.

When you seek out the perspective of others, you avoid the pitfalls and discover new tools that further your success. There's no limit to the possibilities.

Or is there? The reality is, of course, that much of our success is completely out of our control. In the next chapter, we will compare the circumstances we *can* control to the ones we *can't*.

Mindset 4
Circumstances

Focus solely on what you can control. Trying to steer the circumstances out of your control will destroy your chances of success.

● ● ● ● ● ● ● ●

"We can let circumstances rule us, or we can take charge and rule our lives from within."
—Earl Nightingale

E ven in high school I was focused on high achievement. I remember worrying about one test so much that it impacted my sleep and consumed my every thought for days.

Finally, one day I realized I couldn't control what questions the teacher would ask, how much homework was due in other classes, or even whether or not the power would go out the night before, causing my alarm to reset and resulting in me waking up late.

The only thing I could really control was the amount of time I prepared for the test. When I stopped worrying about all the "what if's," I was finally able to take all that energy I spent worrying and put it into studying for the actual test.

There are two types of circumstances: those you can control and those that you can't. The way you view these two types of circumstances, and especially your mindset for approaching the circumstances you *can't* control, directly affect your threshold for success.

However, most people think they have much more control over their circumstances than they do. Within the circumstances and issues throughout the world, there are those issues you are interested or concerned about, but are outside your control, the global economy, for example, national politics, or even the interest rate on your credit card. There is an even smaller group of concerns and issues you do have influence over, for example, the number of sales calls you make, how often you exercise, and how much you study for your licensing tests.

The Circumstances Mindset reminds us that our sphere of concern is bigger than our sphere of control, and that by focusing on the circumstances that are in our control, we can make a much larger impact and become more successful.

Focus on the Ten Percent

You can only control about ten percent of your circumstances (the events in your life). However, most people focus most of their efforts on the ninety percent they **can't** control and end up wasting their time and resources. The truth is, if you focus on the circumstances out of your control, your success will be limited and you will grow discouraged.

As a financial advisor, the market is a constant reminder of my limited ability to control circumstances. I know I can't control the market, so why would I constantly worry about it? It would be more helpful for me to think about what I can control, for example, the amount of research I do or how frequently I communicate with my clients. Not only do I strive to not allow these circumstances to affect me, but I do my best to prepare my clients so that it doesn't affect them either. I remind them that some days they'll wake up and the market will be down. But it's about the bigger picture, and they shouldn't worry about every dip in the market or every bad circumstance that comes along. If my goal is to solve world hunger, that is in my sphere of "concern," but is out of my sphere of "control." But if I changed my focus to a situation within my control, I would be much more effective. I would end up too busy wasting my time with things that I can't actually control. Imagine if I focused on the ten percent. How much more could I accomplish, then?

Some of the greatest sports legends have adopted this mindset. LeBron James[17], for example, was born to a sixteen-year-old mother in a rough neighborhood in New York City. Growing up, James' life was anything but stable. In fourth grade, he moved six times and missed about 100 days of school. He had no idea who his father was except that he was in jail. As a child, James learned to be adaptable. There were a lot of things outside his control, but he focused his energy on the things he could control: himself and his actions. He started playing football and basketball in middle school. He woke up early most mornings to practice. He found the ten percent of his circumstances that he could control and took hold of them at a young age. Although he had plenty of things he could worry about, James' mindset was focused on what he could control and achieved a great deal of success because of it.

When I played basketball in college, I knew I could never control my opponents' jump shots or lay-up skills. I couldn't control how fast they were, or the amount of time they played. I couldn't control the referees either. What could I control in this situation? Myself, how I fostered my abilities, and the way in which I responded to my teammates. When I worked at these, I saw a change in my performance, ability, and success. I practiced longer and harder. Success followed.

The ten percent is the hours spent practicing, the conversations I have with my clients, the preparation for tests, and LeBron's determination.

How do you discover your ten percent? How do you know what is in your control? You need to ask yourself this question: **In this circumstance, what can I control?**

The question is not: What do I *wish* I could control? Or what do I *want* to control? Instead, it is: What **can** I control?

Find out the answer and resolve to reach your full potential in the ten percent.

Ignore the Ninety Percent

When I was growing up, change was a constant. We lived in 5 states and 26 different houses and struggled financially almost everywhere we went. Growing up in this environment, I was constantly waiting for the next shoe to drop. My thoughts were filled with, "maybe's" and "what if's". Not only was I constantly worrying, but I was stressed and unhappy. As a result, other parts of my life suffered.

When you put the majority of your attention on the ninety percent of things that aren't important or that you can't control, you are wasting your most valuable asset: your time.

Worrying won't change anything—it won't lessen the likelihood of the event actually happening. Instead, make the choice to manage your ten percent, and accept the fact that the other ninety percent is outside of your control.

Overcome Your Excuses

When I started my practice, I had every possible excuse to fail: I had only been living in Nashville for a few years and didn't have any kind of personal network to rely on for new clients. Most people only entrust their money to people with grey hair and glasses, but I was just 24 years old with only four years of experience and financial training. Why would anyone listen to *my* advice? I had just left my job and was starting over from nothing in an industry where only one in five advisors last longer than five years.

Older advisors warned me, telling me it would take twenty years to build a business, and I needed to be content with mundane results for years. I ignored them. I just wasn't that patient. What could I control in that situation? The first thing I had to decide was to recognize and overcome the excuses I had been making. In three years, I had built a business that was more successful than almost all the seasoned advisors who had warned me when I was first starting out.

It's easy to list out the circumstances that are holding you back, but in reality, they're just excuses you use to stay comfortable.

The industry tells you, "In 20 years, you can be really successful." You learn that success is a slow process, and yes, you probably can take twenty years to reach a level of success if that's your expectation. But I'm living proof that you can do it faster. I've done in three years what others haven't been able to do in twenty. I know it's possible, because I won't let my circumstances control me or what I do.

An expectation is the belief you have about what you can and will achieve. What you expect will often dictate and control our circumstances, and in turn, your success. You've heard things about yourself and your situation that are not true, and you need to realize it. Instead of allowing others to set expectations for you, set your own expectations. Focus on the few circumstances you can control, master them, and you'll blow past any expectations others set for you.

Excuses are one of success' greatest enemies. If you find yourself saying, "This is the best I can do," I would challenge you to rethink your potential.

In Difficult Circumstances, Do It Anyway

In difficult situations, remember a time where you felt powerful. It will bring back feelings of confidence, and you'll do better.

Just yesterday, I had to speak to forty people I had never met. The stakes were high: if I did well, we might get a new client. If I failed, we would probably lose them. For most of my life, I had a deep fear of public speaking, and while I've gotten a lot better, I found myself getting nervous about this talk. What if I messed up? What if I forgot the material? What if they asked questions I didn't know the answer to? What if the audience hated it, and we lost the client because I couldn't hold their interest?

But as the anxiety came on, I used the Circumstances Mindset. I recognized I had no control over how they might receive our presentation or me. I told myself, "You've done this kind of thing before. You can do this." I made an effort to act comfortably and confidently, even if I didn't feel it. However, people took notice, and the presentation went well.

I still get nervous, even now. I still know there will be questions I won't know the answers to. I still have to look at the screen during the presentation sometimes.

But that's okay. I can't control the questions that are going to be asked, but I can show up on time. I can be prepared. I can know my presentation inside and out.

The Circumstances Mindsets is *designed* for difficult situations. This is where it works best. When you feel anxiety about something you need to do, use it to stop worrying about what could go *wrong* and focus on the two or three things you can control in order to give the best possible chance for it to go *right*.

Set Realistic Expectations

It's not just negative circumstances that affect your success. Positive circumstances can limit you as well.

A few months ago, a fellow advisor was sharing that he had just gained a new client. When I congratulated him, he followed up by outlining his vacation plans. A few weeks after his vacation, I noticed him show up to the office less and less. On the days he did come to the office, he came in late and left early.

What had changed? Why was he suddenly unmotivated?

After watching him for a few weeks, I realized he let the positive circumstance of getting a good deal distract him from building it further. This was partly due to the lack of expectations he had set for himself.

Sometimes, even in positive circumstances, we learn to limit ourselves and settle for believing, "this is the best I can do" or "I don't need to do any better."

You need to ask yourself: **What expectation of work am I setting for myself?**

You have a responsibility to those who depend on you and also to your true potential to do the best you can. You have a limited amount of time. Will you spend it doing as little as possible, or will you push yourself to grow even further?

Circumstances in Action:

Make a list of the circumstances that are you are concerned with. Then, identify which of those circumstances are within your *control*. Shift your focus and activity to those. If you focus on these, the possibilities are endless.

Despite your circumstances, your end goal is still achievable. Sometimes our circumstances aren't easy or comfortable. Should we avoid those uncomfortable situations? In our next chapter, I'll prove that by embracing discomfort, you will grow faster and more than you thought was possible.

Mindset 5
Discomfort

If you avoid discomfort, success will avoid you in return. Accomplish uncomfortable things to increase your capacity for greatness and achieve your true potential. When you press into discomfort, you will find yourself alone at the head of the pack.

● ● ● ● ● ● ●

You know what you want, and maybe you have a plan to get there, but what makes you different from everyone else? Why should a client come to you over the guy down the street?

If you don't know, neither will your customers.

Almost everyone can do the basics of a sales job. It's easy to get by while doing the bare minimum. All it takes is showing up, cold calling people, sending generic letters and boring spam emails. It's easy to ask family and friends for referrals and then get enough business to live fairly comfortably, even if you're not making that much of an impact on the world.

But I don't believe you are reading this book because you want that kind of mediocre success.

There is a popular saying, "If it doesn't challenge you, it won't change you." That is what Rapid, Top-Level Success is—embracing mindsets and things we've never done to obtain results that we have never had.

There's a reason you've never done the things that will allow you to achieve Rapid, Top-Level Success: they are uncomfortable. It's easier to stick to simpler tasks, those things you're "supposed to do," the things everyone does, but when you do that, you will find yourself settling for just getting by.

So what are you going to do? I can assure you it will not be sending more generic emails, asking your friends for more referrals, or hanging out by the water cooler. Doing what it takes to really achieve success will not be easy or comfortable. If you want Rapid, Top-Level Success, though, you need something else, something harder, less comfortable. You need a different mindset.

Misogi Accomplishes the Impossible

In 2014, Atlanta Hawks basketball player, Kyle Korver had one of the best seasons of his life. Over an 80+ game NBA season[18], he shot 49.2 percent from the three-point line, making 221 three-pointers. He was often called the best shooter in the NBA that year. How did he maintain that high level of excellence so consistently over an 80+ game NBA season? What was the secret of his success?

The summer before the 2014 season, Korver participated in what he called a Misogi[19]. Misogi is, historically, an ancient Japanese ritual of cleansing, but the concept has been modified to challenge people in extreme circumstances.

Kyle Korver's misogi was to run a 5K. Not too difficult, right? Except the 5K was underwater. In the ocean. Without an oxygen mask. While carrying a boulder weighing about 100 pounds. He would swim to the ocean floor, pick up the boulder, run as long as he could while holding his breath, drop the boulder, and return to the surface to tread water while he caught his breath to go do it again.

The concept of misogi can be summed up as this: **take on a challenge that radically expands your idea of what is possible.**

Marcus Elliot, the founder of modern-day misogi and Harvard-trained sports scientist says, "It's not a ride at Disneyland or a Tough Mudder, it's a personal quest designed by you. And it's really hard. You have a 50 percent chance of success, at best."

The lesson that the misogi teaches its students is that they are capable of much more than they ever imagined. It is only through extreme challenge that someone can realize their full potential.

"If it's hard enough, the lesson will last," says Elliott.

How to Embrace Discomfort

The Mindset of Discomfort is about choosing to embrace new, challenging situations, and as a result, growing in ways you didn't know were possible. Growth itself is impossible without discomfort. To reach the next level of success, growth is necessary. If you don't chose to embrace discomfort and grow now, you'll be stuck doing the comfortable, easy things because you don't know you can do any better.

Not all uncomfortable challenges need to be physical. Right now, my misogi is the words on these pages. It's writing a book. Before I started this project, I thought to myself, "What's the most uncomfortable thing I could do next?" I thought, "Ha, probably write a book or something." And then I realized this wasn't something to laugh about. That really was the next challenge I needed to embrace.

I don't know anything about writing or publishing a book. To be honest, I started this process a little unsure that I could ever accomplish anything like this. Over the last few months, however, I've begun to realize I can accomplish more than I ever imagined. That's the purpose of a challenge, to redefine what is possible.

The most uncomfortable situation is what will get you to realize that your potential is so much greater than you think it is. You can do and become more, than you think you can. And as you approach challenges, regardless of whether you succeed or not, you'll discover you can do more than you ever imagined.

I want to challenge you to creating a misogi of your own. What if you made your misogi, your almost impossible challenge, your personal success goal? You may not know exactly how you're going to succeed, but during the process, you'll find you will come out better on the other side for trying.

Accept the Challenge

You have two options when it comes to discomfort. You can either choose to accept and embrace the challenge, or you can spend most your time avoiding it. You can live in fear of the discomfort, or realize that it is the only thing that will push you further and make you more successful.

To be fair, both ways can work. Activity delivers results. However, easy, unfocused, comfortable activity will breed low level success, whereas if you want Rapid, Top-Level Success, you need challenging, ultra-focused, *un*comfortable activity.

And when you choose to accept the challenge, a transformation happens in your mind. Instead of spending your time fighting the discomfort, you stop and decide that you are willing to accept whatever it takes, even if it's uncomfortable. Suddenly, the question changes from, "*Can* I do this?" to, "*How* do I do this?"

Yes, you will still have to do the hard work, but the mindset shift makes all the difference between achieving your goal and giving up. Soon, you stop focusing on how awful and hard the challenge is. You can even start to enjoy it.

When your mindset changes to accepting and embracing the discomfort, your success changes too. When your clients and customers see that you not only serve them well, but are willing to make uncomfortable choices, they will trust you more. The focus on serving the needs of your clients, even if it's not easy or comfortable, is what will separate you from your competitors in your industry.

Intentional Discomfort

There's a difference between embracing discomfort and masochism. I don't want you to think that when I embrace discomfort I love it. It's often hard, but I choose short-term pain because I know it will lead to long term-success. If you're going to embrace discomfort, you want to make sure you are intentional about the choices you make.

I choose discomfort by running it past my Future Self. I remind myself of who I want to be in five years and ask myself, **"What do I need to do to get there?"** The honest answer to this question is never an easy nor comfortable one.

The kind of discomfort we need to embrace is the kind that will always push us to grow. These uncomfortable decisions produce a more positive outcome. Our discomfort should always be pushing us closer to our Future Self.

If you are going to embrace discomfort, you want to know that it is the most efficient discomfort you can take on. A few years ago, I was faced with a choice to pursue discomfort or settle for what I had.

I used to *hate* public speaking. I would avoid it at all costs. Then about two years ago, I realized that in order to take my own success to the next level, I would need to get over that fear. I had the opportunity to start gaining clients by speaking to larger groups and teaching them about what financial advisors could do for them. I knew these opportunities would bring my success to a whole new level, but dreaded the thought of getting in front of them.

I started researching a few different classes and seminars that would help me improve my public speaking. I found a few that met weekly or monthly, but that was too easy, and I didn't want to wait months to improve my public speaking. After a little more research I found a three-day intensive program. Even the idea of speaking for three full days terrified me. It required a lot more work and potential discomfort, however, the results promised to be huge.

I signed up, and when the program came, I spent three days speaking, getting in front of a panel who watched and critiqued our speeches, videotaping our talks, and then watching the videos to see how we did. It was horrible. However, I grew more in those three days than I would have in months of once a week meetings. It was the most uncomfortable thing to do, but it was the fastest and best way to accomplish my goal, and I learned again that when you decide to embrace discomfort, you can speed up and amplify your growth toward your full potential.

When to Stop

You need to be aware of when to stop doing something that isn't working.

I wouldn't have the success I do today if I hadn't embraced discomfort and tried new things. But I also wouldn't have the success I do now if I kept pressing into things that just didn't work. We must come to the realization that not everything we try is going to work, and sometimes we need to change the methods we use.

Before the Wright[20] brothers flew an airplane for the first time, they experimented with hundreds of other techniques while they perfected their first flight. They tried implementing different wing styles and methods of steering and tried them repeatedly. When they came across a style that didn't work, they went back to the drawing board, determined to find a better method.

We, like the Wright brothers, have to be honest with ourselves with what works and what doesn't. That way, we can spend our time, energy, and focus on the things that *do* work and bring us closer to our goal.

It's good to press into discomfort for growth, but when you stop seeing results or growth, it might be time to find a new challenge.

The Path of Least Resistance

We so often try to find the easiest path to get where we want to go, but there comes a time when you need to choose between the easy path and the best path.

In my junior year of college, I decided I wanted to be a Financial Advisor. I remember thinking to myself, *"What can I be doing now to increase my chances of success after I graduate?"*

I knew that my answer depended greatly on my willingness to do uncomfortable things.

This awareness led me to the library many nights of my senior year to self-study for my license exams. I didn't go to Mexico for Spring Break like a lot of people I knew were doing. I knew that I was sacrificing now so that I could be more successful in the future.

I have a friend who always wanted to go back to school to get his Masters in Law. He has now reached a certain point in his career where he can't go any further because he didn't pursue the education he needed. He tells me now, "I wish I had done the hard thing when I had the chance." Now, with a family and kids, he's fairly successful and happy, but he still wishes he could do more. The same situation happened with another friend who told me, "I wish I hadn't switched from studying medicine because now I'm stuck." He traded the discomfort for an easier degree, and now wishes he had stuck with the more uncomfortable one because it could have brought him so much further.

It's not that they can't go back to school, or figure out another way to reach the success they wanted, but now, with families and responsibilities, the path is a lot more difficult and complicated.

The more time you spend avoiding discomfort, the higher the stakes get.

The longer you avoid the discomfort, the more opportunities you risk missing. The longer you wait, the harder the path will get. Your attempt to prevent discomfort will backfire.

I understand that not many of you will know in your college years what you want your career path to look like, and even if you do, it will most likely change. But I do know that even in the midst of uncertainty, if you continue to press into and embrace discomfort, you will learn you can do anything. And most often I've found if you choose to avoid the discomfort, you'll regret taking the easy path.

Discomfort is a Choice

You have the power to choose how you approach discomfort.

You can plead ignorance by saying, "If I had known, I would have done it. I just didn't know." Or you can take the first step. The first step to get uncomfortable is asking uncomfortable questions about yourself and your business.

What is the most uncomfortable thing I can do to grow my business right now?

Changing your mindset to embrace discomfort is deciding you want to continually grow and get better. Choosing to embrace discomfort is choosing to pursue your full potential.

Is It Worth It?

For a lot of you the question isn't, "How do I embrace discomfort?" But you're saying to yourself, "Why change something if it's working? It might not be the best, but I'm comfortable and making enough to get by."

And perhaps you're right. There is no reason for you to embrace hard situations and be uncomfortable. There might be no pressing burden.

However, I believe that you have the ability to reach your full potential, and by choosing to settle for the comfortable lifestyle, by doing the bare minimum, you will *never* reach your full potential.

Discomfort in Action:

Take a few minutes and come up with three ideas for your "misogi." Look back to your future self and compare your potential "misogi" to your future self. Which one lines up best with who you want to be and will push you hardest to reach your future self? Do that.

When you do uncomfortable things, you will discover how much more you can accomplish. You will gain confidence, and in turn, become more successful. When you reach your full potential, I have the feeling you'll realize you can do even better.

Speaking of discomfort, some of the most uncomfortable situations are those involving conflict. I've seen hundreds of books talk about conflict, but none like this. In the next chapter, we'll explore the *real* goal behind conflict and how it can change your life.

Mindset 6
Conflict

Conflict is a tool to further your business goals. Use conflict to better understand your clients and colleagues, not as a fight to win. However, conflict can also reveal business relationships that need to end.

● ● ● ⬤ ● ● ●

Although avoiding conflict often seems easier than confronting it, avoidance only brings more confusion to your business relationships. Healthy conflict allows you to gain new perspective, and if you can learn how to do conflict well, your business relationships will be strengthened.

When you embrace the path to success, you are at the same time inviting conflict into your life. When you begin to be successful, you slowly stop becoming a "one-man show" and will find yourself needing more help. The more people are involved, the more beliefs and emotions that are added to your life, the more variables to affect your success, whether positively or negatively. At this point, conflict will be inevitable and necessary, and the discomfort and hard conversations become much more valuable. The goal of success and growing your business is worth the conflict.

If one of your team members had an approach toward clients that turned them away or miscommunicated your values and business practices, would you want them to continue? Or would you rather confront their approach so the issue could be fixed? In the pursuit to become successful, you will be faced with these conflicts often.

Why We Come into Conflict

Conflict happens. However, the Conflict Mindset reminds us that conflict is not something to be feared. Instead, conflict is a tool.

Dealing with other people's money is a lot more than dealing with numbers. Clients sometimes get confused about different fees and unexpected downturns in the market. However, when a client calls me frustrated about some dip in the market or a fee statement, I've realized that's not really the issue. In these awkward conversations, I've found clients are actually afraid. They're afraid of the markets crashing, their money disappearing, and their security being taken from them. Dealing with someone's money is emotional and conflict is often a sign that the clients are worried about their future.

About a year ago, I got into a conflict with one of my best clients. We had invested some of his money into bonds and had already made about $100,000, but with the markets, as unpredictable as they are, the profit went down to $90,000 a few weeks later.

My client called me furious, "How can we be losing money!?" he asked. "Once you make money, you shouldn't be able to just lose it like that!"

I tried to explain that we have no control over the markets. "This is still $90,000-$100,000 you would have never made if we hadn't put your money in these bonds."

He was still confused and upset, and so I asked him and his wife to meet with me in my office.

"So let's talk about your account," I told him when we met later that week.

He began to explain how he was watching it daily and didn't understand how we could have $100,000 one month and then only $90,000 the next.

"You can't have the expectation of always making money, "I tried explaining. "The markets fluctuate and so will the account because of that."

He began questioning if I really knew what I was doing.

"If this is going to be a continuing conversation we keep having, we may need to consider the possibility that we might not be able to continue working together," I told him calmly.

"No, that's not what we mean. We're just worried. We just wanted to make sure someone was watching our account."

As we continued the conversation, I shifted my questions to figure out what they were *really* worried about, and soon

I was able to address those concerns. In that moment, figuring out what was best for the client was my goal, even if that meant the end of our business relationship. The only way to come to this conclusion was to confront the issues head on.

Through the conflict with that client, I discovered that the real issue had nothing to do with the $10,000 that fluctuated. The clients wanted to make sure that I was paying attention to their accounts and that their money was in good hands. They wanted to know that they could trust me.

So by having this confrontation, I could share with them the reality of the business and how it works. Then they were able to readjust their expectations of me. I was only able to do this because I sought the facts over winning the confrontation. If my goal was to win in this moment, I'm positive I would have lost my client.

The Goal of Conflict in Business

When I have a client call me and confront me about a certain investment or account, I know now that I need to seek the root behind the problem in order to resolve the conflict.

The goal behind these kinds of conflicts—and any conflict in business—cannot be to win. I'm not saying that you never *will* "win," but if winning is your goal, you will not achieve Rapid, Top-Level Success.

When you enter conflict with the goal of winning, you become close-minded, willing to do anything to prove you're right. You might win the conflict, but you could lose your client's business or your team members respect. Because conflict can be emotional, it is important that the real goal behind our conflict be **to fact find**.

I previously entered confrontations with the desire to be right, but I knew that mindset wasn't going to get me anywhere with my clients. My goal shifted from trying to win, to trying to find the facts of the situation.

When your goal in the conflict is to fact find, you become open to growth and new perspectives. When you begin to have conflict centered around gaining new perspective, you *avoid* conflict in the future because you learn what people want and need before problems arise. I've avoided many conflicts, and lessened the impact of others, because I learned to seek perspective and find the facts before confrontation was necessary.

Don't Avoid Conflict

In my family, we go all in for conflict. We've been through so much together, and we recognize the benefit of being honest with one another even if it's not something the other person wants to hear. We've created an intimacy and depth in our relationships this way. I've observed that people who avoid conflict to save relationships actually end up with more shallow relationships.

Avoiding conflict can be dangerous for business owners, or anyone who wants to be successful. When you avoid conflict, you are missing out on the perspectives of others and end up avoiding areas in which you can improve. Success is very rarely an act of solitude. When you're working with others, avoiding conflict often leads to feelings of bitterness towards others and future blowouts.

On my team, we've learned to start embracing conflict more regularly. When the team was first formed, everyone liked to agree on everything because we didn't know each other well. The "honeymoon phase" ended, though, and we soon realized we don't always agree on everything. However, I saw it as a good and necessary thing. Trust is built when you resolve conflicts. When conflict is avoided, you end up with shallow relationships that won't withstand the toughest situations. Every week, I ask my team hard questions to make sure they're operating at their full potential.

When advisors lose clients, it's often not because they're not handling their money well. It's because conflict and hard conversations are avoided. When clients are confused about fees or market downturns, hard conversations are easy to avoid, but if you do, clients can feel taken advantage of and may leave the relationship.

Conflict Gives You Perspective

I've mentioned how conflict is about "gaining perspective", but I want to take a minute and really focus on what that looks like.

In 2015, there was a controversy that went viral over the color of a dress in a picture. Some people said it was clearly blue and black, while others claimed it was definitely white and gold. Some people were so determined that they were right that they did studies and even searches for the actual dress. This is the perfect example of why gaining perspective is so important. Something as small as the color of a dress can be seen drastically differently, and if we want the whole picture, we need to invite others to show us their perspective.

Sometimes I get into conflict and discover that my perspective was off. It took being in the conflict and coming out of it to actually recognize that.

Despite who's right or wrong, you have to be able to see where the other person was coming from and where it originated. You can only do that if they tell you or show you.

It's like looking at a drawing or painting, but not knowing what it means or even what it is. Then the painter says, "Let me show you my perspective." They have the ability to point out shapes you overlooked or hidden messages in the artwork that you weren't able to see from your perspective. That's what conflict does, shows you the inner workings of another person's mind. It reveals how someone else sees the world and prepares you to look at things differently.

If you are in a healthy situation and the conflict is handled well, not only will you gain perspective, but so will the other person. When you can share your thoughts and beliefs, others will better understand you and where you were coming from in this conflict. The benefits to gaining perspective outweigh the temporary discomfort of conflict.

Choosing Appropriate Conflict

I used to think that all conflict was beneficial and appropriate, but over the last few years I've found there are times that you choose conflict, and times you realize it's better to not confront someone.

Last year, I had an assistant for four months and it was not working out. She didn't seem like she cared about the clients or business. She wasn't willing to learn. Despite being presented with multiple opportunities for growth, she never took them. Because the financial business is an ever-changing industry, that kind of attitude wasn't what I was looking for. I decided to fire her. I brought her into my office and gave her the news and asked her, "Do you want to know why it didn't work out?"

She responded, "No," but I thought she had a lot of potential and wanted her to know how she could improve, so I told her.

"You seem like you don't care and don't really want to grow. I need someone in this environment who is willing to learn and eager to take on new responsibilities."

She left my office and about an hour later I got a phone call from her husband saying that she had come home crying and that I had been unnecessarily mean to her. I knew that I hadn't, but it didn't matter, because that's how she perceived the situation.

This is when I realized that she wasn't ready for perspective. The conflict only did more damage than it helped. Were the things I told her true? Yes. Did me telling her those things help her? No.

This situation helped me realize that not everyone is ready for conflict. Choosing appropriate conflict is important in maintaining relationships.

If you don't stop to evaluate whether a conflict is an appropriate one, you will be fighting most of your life. You can always find something to disagree about, but that is not going to bring you any closer to success.

To choose appropriate conflict, there are a few questions you need to ask:

- Will conflict lead to a solution?
- Will this conflict help solidify a relationship now or down the road?
- Am I going into this conflict with the goal to win or fact-find?

I believe that conflict is necessary to resolve problems, but if there is nothing to gain from the conflict, you need to double check your motives.

Don't make the same mistake I did and approach someone who is not ready for conflict. If they are not willing to come into the discussion with an open mind, the conflict will often bring more harm than good. Sometimes the step you need to take before having conflict is to explain to the person the benefits and real goal behind the conflict.

In Conflict, It's All About Relationship

In a sales position, we have conflict with clients and team members. Both situations are handled differently, but I believe the desired result in both scenarios are the same. When our conflicts involve multiple relationships with others, our desired result is to maintain these relationships while coming to a compromise or solution.

When I was new to the financial advisor business, I believed that I was simply dealing with money and that my goal was to help people make more money. I quickly realized that the business is much more about building and maintaining relationships.

In sales, *you* are the product. Your customers are not just buying your products, they're buying you. People won't buy a house with a realtor they don't trust, just like someone won't trust the plan I develop for them if they don't trust *me*. Relationships are at the core of success, and navigating conflict is essential to relationships.

After being honest with the client who was concerned about the drop in their account balance, I could see that they began to trust me more. When they saw that I was willing to have a hard conversation with them, it solidified our relationship. They respected me more because they were then able to understand where I was coming from and what I was going to do for them. I understood where they were coming from and how I could best communicate with them. We both learned how to best navigate the relationship. We only learned these things that strengthened our relationship through conflict.

That conversation bore practical fruit, too. Not long afterward, they referred a new client to me. The conflict led directly to a greater degree of success.

This concept is even more important in relationships with members of your team.

The most successful teams are the ones that have gone through the most together and learned that they can trust one another. That's why even when you're *right* in a conflict, you still need to remember that the purpose of conflict is to maintain and build relationships. This is why team building is emphasized so highly in military team training.

6 Tips to Use Conflict Well in Your Business

After several years of embracing the conflict mindset, I've found that there are a few key points behind successful conflict. It's easy to go into conflict angry, yelling, and hurting a lot of relationships along the way. Here are six tips to do conflict well.

Stay Calm. I recently had an advisor come into my office, storm around, yell a lot, and not accomplish much. I sat at my desk and let him finish. I calmly started asking him questions and getting to the bottom of what he was actually upset about. Only when he calmed down and started explaining himself were we able to reach an understanding and solution. When you're angry or upset, you can enter fight-or-flight mode. You start trying to fight and win, but nothing really gets accomplished. You can often end up saying things you later regret. Staying calm is essential to get anywhere in conflict.

Seek the Cause. The cause of a conflict is often very different than what the actual confrontation is about. In my business, I've often found that people are afraid of not having enough money to live or retire, so they argue about fees or the markets. When I address the root issue/cause head on, I am able to resolve and even avoid potential conflicts.

Ask Questions and Listen. Don't lead with your opinions and try to prove you're right when you're in conflict. One of the secrets to successful conflict is asking questions and listening. Most conflict is either a miscommunication or about something completely different than the argument at hand. The only way to find the root of the problem is to ask questions and listen in-between the lines.

Remember the Real Goal. The real goal behind successful conflict is not to win, but to fact find. Conflict can often be emotional and facts can often be forgotten or overlooked. The facts don't lie and can often bring clarity to a situation that needs it.

Face-to-Face. When I have to have a conflict with a client or team member, I always make sure to have it face-to-face. Conflicts over email or phone can often be one-sided and make it difficult to really understand the other person. Body language, eye contact, and physical atmosphere are important in being able to connect with and maintain relationship. It's easy to say harsh things over email or on the phone when you can't see the other person. Face-to-face conflicts are always more successful than trying to communicate over the phone or through email.

Take Time. In the past, I was always willing to confront the conflict right away. I thought, "If you have a problem, let's talk about it right now." I've learned that with many people, it's best to take time before having this confrontation. When you take the time to think about the situation, you are often able to gain more perspective. It's also good to not get into conflict when people are emotional and instead give time for them to be in a relaxed, calm state.

Conflict is often seen in a negative light, as something to be avoided in business and in your personal life. However, the Conflict Mindset says avoiding conflict can bring about feelings of distrust and miscommunication in business. Instead, use conflict skillfully to further your goals.

When Relationships Need to End

Just like conflict is used to reinforce relationships, it is also a tool for evaluating if other business relationships are right. Not all business relationships work, it's important to know which ones don't and end them.

Of course, you can't toss people aside because they've made you uncomfortable. I ask myself, "**What's a reasonable amount of conflict and discomfort and hard conversations to have being in this business?**"

A few years ago, I was working with a large client who owned several hardware stores outside of Memphis. As we went through our initial evaluation, he avoided most of my questions. He told me bits and pieces of his financial situation, but some of this information he gave was contradictory. I was left confused.

After several meetings, we finally got all the information we needed and began creating a plan for him, but when we delivered the plan to him, he asked me to run it by an advisor whom he had worked with previously and who was now retired. At the client's request, I spoke with the advisor, and all of a sudden he decided to come out of retirement and accused me of stealing his client. He then demanded all the work I had done over the last few months.

I confronted him and told him we could work together, but it ended up not working that way. The other advisor ended up taking the work I had done, still accusing me of stealing his client, and made $120,000 from the deal. The client told us he still wanted to work with my team but also wanted the other advisor involved.

I tried to navigate this situation. Who would want to walk away from a year's worth of work? I continually tried to involve the advisor and finish the process.

The months leading to finishing the deal were filled with confusion and miscommunication. My team and I were working hard to close out the stressful deal. When we finally finished, the other advisor took 70 percent of the profit, while I split the remaining 30 percent with another advisor on my team who helped us. It was a draining year-long ordeal.

At one point, I sat across from the 65-year-old "retired" advisor and confronted him. It was the most stressful part of a stressful situation. He was 35 years my senior, and I had no idea how he was going to respond.

"You're not telling me the whole truth," I told him. "The stories you're telling me are different from what you're telling the client. What am I missing?"

He continued to give me excuses and vague answers. I decided in that moment that if he was not going to be honest with me, it was not worth my time or energy to continue this relationship, even though it was profitable financially.

At the time, I tried to follow my own mindset. *What will this conflict accomplish?* I asked myself. I realized then that conflict can help you reveal whether a relationship is worth continuing. In this case, it clearly wasn't.

After the deal closed, the advisor told me, "We want to keep you on and slowly transfer the business over to you over the next two years."

I politely, but quickly responded, "No thank you." I knew the stress and confusion of this entire process was not worth it.

Being able to engage in conflict will help you see that the amount of stress, time, and confrontation that comes with some relationships is not worth it. You might be able to see that eventually anyway, but conflict speeds up the process because it reveals someone's true character.

Conflict in Action:

Is there a potential conflict you have been avoiding? A hard conversation you should have with a team member? Evaluate whether this is an appropriate conflict, using the questions from the "Choosing Appropriate Conflict" section. If so, have the conversation using the "6 Tips to Use Conflict Well in Your Business."

Embracing the appropriate conflict can solidify relationships and speed up success. The uncomfortable and hard conversations have proved worth it for my business. When we see conflict as a tool to gain perspective and understand others better, we are given a chance to improve our businesses, our success, and ourselves.

We've gone through six mindsets that will completely revolutionize your success and change your life if you use them. But how are you going to implement these mindsets? Well, our next chapter will talk about time balance and how to make our time intentional and effective. You can't become successful if you have no time to do it.

Mindset 7
Time Balance

Intentional time can be one of your most powerful tools. Learn how the most successful people accomplish so much more than the average person when given the same amount of time.

● ● ● ● ● ● ●

"The bad news is time flies. The good news is you're the pilot."
—Michael Altshuler

No matter who you are, despite your race, gender, career, or salary, you have a limited amount of time in your life. Twenty-four hours each day to decide how you spend it. Time is your most valuable asset, and the choices you make about how to use it will determine whether you actually achieve success.

Real Time vs. Clock Time

There are actually two different kinds of time: real time and clock time. Clock time is the sixty seconds in every minute, the sixty minutes in every hour, and the 24 hours in every day. Clock time is measured equally. Real time is relative, dragging on or flying by, often dependent on what we're doing.

Last week when I stood in line at the DMV, time dragged. It only took an hour, but it felt like I had been there for days. The twelve minutes in each quarter of a basketball game is *clock* time, each minute accounted for by sixty seconds. The several days I spent in line at the DMV, even though it was only an hour, is *real* time.

We live in a world run on clock time, but our minds run on *real* time. It's a lot easier to manage clock time. We can schedule and plan our allotted minutes all we want, but when real time kicks in, tasks can take longer than you anticipate, minutes fly by faster than you can count.

For me, the first three hours of the day go by the fastest, and I often get the most done, whereas the last three hours, from two to five each day, are often the hardest. I usually schedule meetings or activities that involve other people in this time so that I am forced to be more productive. You need to determine what your *real time* looks like and how to leverage it.

The Two Sides of the Time Balance Spectrum

One example of a time balance situation most of us walk by daily is the water cooler. When I was first growing my business, I found out people perceived me as "not very friendly." It's not because I didn't like my team members, it was because I wouldn't take the time to stop and talk to people in the office. I wouldn't hang out by the water cooler to talk about last night's game or how the market was performing that day. When I was at the office, I worked head-down, non-stop every second of every day.

When people would say hi or stop me to talk, I would be counting the seconds in my head, thinking *this is a waste of time. I don't have time to talk to you about how your kids are doing.* Yes, I sound like a jerk, but that's not the point. My priority at the office was to get work done, and that's a good priority to have.

However, you have to balance your priorities with your relationships with others. The way I was living is one end of the Time Balance spectrum. I see the other end of the spectrum every time I leave my office to grab something from the printer or walk to the fridge: a few guys hanging around the proverbial "water cooler," shooting the breeze, cracking jokes, and complaining about the market. I hear them every time I walk by. This is the far other side of the spectrum.

Somewhere between the water cooler dwellers and the "workaholics," there is a balance.

I only found this balance after becoming a leader. I'm finding how valuable it is to talk to my team members and business partners. Not only can I learn from their perspective, but they are more effective when they know they have a boss who actually cares more about them than the tasks they're performing. I still don't talk for hours at the water cooler, but I have slowly developed deeper relationships by taking time away from my work to show I care about them.

Success Follows Intentionality

I used to think that the amount of time I spent on something directly correlated the amount of success it would produce. Then I found that it's not about the amount of "clock time," but the amount of "real time" or intentional time.

Intentional time is the deliberate, purposeful way you spend your time. Standing in a garage next to a car for five hours doesn't make you a mechanic, but studying car manuals and being intentional about learning the trade will get you closer.

In your work, you could spend 12 hours a day at your desk, but if you're not being intentional with your time, you might be wasting it.

The more I've grown my business and interacted with other advisors, the more I've seen a common belief that by simply spending a lot of time in the office will make you successful. But spending 12 hours at your desk won't bring you much closer to your desired level of success unless they are 12 *intentional* hours. You can often double your output when you begin to use your time intentionally

The company Cross-Fit is so successful because their methodology centers on intense, intentional time. Compared to regular workouts, Cross-Fit workouts are much more effective in much less time.

To help create intentional time, plan out the next day the night before. This allows you to mentally prepare for the next day, and when you're prepared, it removes the stress about what to do next.

When you create intentional time, you also recognize how much more you can fit into each day of "clock time." I often have a list of things I can be working on when I find myself between meetings and need something I can pick up and put back down again.

Another habit of intentional time is to take advantage of your *thoughts*. The only thing you can take with you no matter where you go are your thoughts. How you use the time you have to *think is easy to overlook*. When you are using your time intentionally, though, you can focus your thoughts productively. I've challenged my team to begin focusing their thoughts on revenue generating activity during work hours, and we've found this simple change to result in more client meetings, ideas, and business.

When creating intentional time, it's important to remember your future self. When you think about where you want to be in a few years, it serves as an incredible motivator for being intentional with your time. It will also help you see the bigger picture behind tasks that might seem hard to be intentional with.

When Priorities Conflict

One of the hardest things for me in my business is conflicting priorities. I want to be the best I can be in my business, but if I were to completely focus on achieving that goal, I would have to make sacrifices in my relationship with my family.

When I first discovered the concept of intentional time, I realized if I spent enough intentional time focused on a single goal, it would most likely succeed. It's an amazing thing. Activity produces results, and intentional activity produces compounded results.

However, I also know the more I focus on one goal, the more the other priorities in my life will suffer. When I first got into this business, I was fresh out of college with little responsibility and what felt like endless time. I worked 12 hour days, six to seven days a week, and poured everything I had into improving myself as a financial advisor.

Then I fell in love and got married—all while making the hard decision to leave the successful firm I was previously working for to pursue a business of my own. Talk about conflicting priorities!

There will come a time when you might not be able to do all the things you want. You may not be able to go back to school like I was able to. You might not be able to work 12 hours a day to launch your business and achieve Rapid, Top-level Success. Your priorities will conflict and you will have to choose how you spend your time.

To be honest, I've found that Rapid, Top-Level Success, or at least the startup phase of success, is nearly impossible if you have conflicting priorities. When I was getting started, my wife and I had to sacrifice a lot. We couldn't buy certain things or go certain places because our priority was preparing for the future success of our family and business.

Remember Steve? His priorities were sleeping in, having a lot of spare time to hang out with friends, and being extremely successful. However, success doesn't work like that, and I believe that's part of the reason he lasted only a few months.

But what if you have a family? Can people with demanding priorities such as having a family achieve Rapid, Top-Level success? Yes, but it takes some sacrifice from your family, not to mention their buy-in. For me, it's imperative to my success to not spend 35 years building an extremely successful business and miss out on my family. I would rather be slightly less successful in my business in order to be successful in my family life. That's why it's time *balance*.

The reason I'm so passionate about using my work time intentionally and balancing work and family is because I've seen the effects of imbalance. My biological father worked long hours for 35 years and didn't understand the idea of balance at that stage of his life. He valued impressing others which, for him, looked like working long hours and not focusing on his family. My mom wasn't willing to wait for him to figure that out and raise four kids by herself in the meantime. And although he didn't lose his family, it looks different now than it may have if there had been *more* balance.

If you don't have this balance and if work takes too much of your time and energy, you will end up losing out on other great parts of life. It's when I saw the effects it's had on my own family, I promised myself I would never let that happen. I don't think you want that to happen either. That's why using your work time to be extremely intentional is so important—so that at the end of the day you can go home to your family or friends and be successful there as well.

This was one of the most important lessons I've ever learned. This is part of *my* success: my family. If your future self goal is to simply make a lot of money, then you can tailor your time balance around that. But something in me thinks that there's something in all of us that wants this balance in *different* areas of our life.

Eliminate Distractions and Inefficient Tasks

Balancing your time often involves eliminating distractions and inefficient tasks. Distractions in our day and age are *endless*: social media, the buzzing phone in your pocket, and the constant email "pings." For some of us, the birds outside are enough to distract us. In order to get the maximum work finished, I've learned how to eliminate my distractions.

Embrace the Time Balance Mindset by admitting eliminating distractions is possible. I used to think that every time I heard my email "ping" or saw the notification, I needed to check my email. I'm finding that the emails will still be in my inbox in a few hours, and that I can be a lot more productive when I don't stop every few minutes to answer an email. Same with the ringing phone. It's okay to not answer every phone call.

This rule is important in business, but also for success in relationships. My wife and I created a rule when we first started dating not to look at our phones when we're at a restaurant together. In every situation, eliminating distractions helps us focus on the task at hand. We're more in control of our distractions than we think.

Another habit of the Time Balance Mindset is specialization, the act of recognizing which tasks you actually need to do and which tasks you can delegate to others. I rarely work on client paperwork or call my clients for our six week follow because my assistant can do that. When I need to somehow create more time for myself or when I find myself with too many things on my list, I ask myself, "What things don't require my expertise or licenses to do?" And I give those things away.

Learn to say no. I've gotten to the place in my business where sometimes I need to have hard conversations with clients about the time they require of me. I recently had to fire a client because of unnecessary time expectations. The client constantly wanted me to communicate with them each time the market changed. They required so much of my time that I realized I had to tell them I could no longer be their financial advisor. When you're first starting out, you'll put up with anything, but as your success grows, you realize how valuable your time is in these situations and can afford to make these hard decisions.

Count the Cost

Being successful comes with a cost. It takes time, effort, and focus. Each of us only have so many resources that we can give to the different priorities in our lives.

A long time ago, I came to the conclusion that I was not going to manage the most assets of any financial advisor in the country. Don't get me wrong, I think that I could if I tried, but I have no desire to be the best because I know it would cost everything. Every minute and every spare thought would go towards striving to be the best. I don't think Michael Jordan was the best at anything besides basketball, because being the best took it all. It took every second and spare thought he had.

I want to be successful and get closer to my full potential every day, but I'm not willing to sacrifice everything else so that I can be the best financial advisor in the country. To me, that is not true success. I'm not willing to sacrifice my marriage and kids for this business.

So as you begin to balance your time, I would challenge you to count the cost beforehand. Remind yourself of who you want to be in five years, and decide what you're willing to sacrifice to get there. This is where you'll find the best balance for you.

Time Balance in Action:
Go through a typical day in your head. Identify the different things you spend time doing (work, family, gym, sports, friends, etc.). Which of these are not bringing you closer to your idea of success, but take up your time? Consider dropping that.

You have almost everything you need to be successful. The last thing we need to look at is the motivation for your success. This journey isn't easy, and if you don't have something motivating you, you'll give up when it gets hard. The next chapter we'll talk about what kinds of motivations work best and how to stay motivated.

Motivation Behind Success: Generosity

● ● ● ● ● ● ●

T hroughout this book, I've introduced seven mindsets that have helped me attain Rapid, Top-Level success. I believe if you follow them, your life will be changed, and you will quickly see the results of your hard work.

But you might wonder why? Why bother with all of these mindsets and hard work?

The problem that I've found with success is that the achievement, goals, and money will only motivate you for so long. I've set—and later met—countless goals on my journey to success. When I look back at the end of the year, I realize that without my true motivation, gaining the money and awards are nice but ultimately meaningless.

If you're like me, you want to spend your life doing something that has a positive effect on the world. By stopping to ask, "why," you can make sure that you are motivated by more than just external incentives. And when you find the answer, you will be motivated to endure a much longer, harder journey toward success.

I've seen many advisors give everything they had to "make it" to the next level, and sacrifice a lot on the way. Being solely motivated by achievement is going to burn you out fast. The constant attempt to achieve more never leads to satisfaction. What is enough? When can you slow down or stop? The pressure advisors put on themselves to achieve is enormous. Then what happens? They give up. It's too much, too hard, and they can't stand the achievement-motivated success.

This was the end result with the advisor Steve. He started off with high goals, but when he didn't meet a goal he set, he grew discouraged. The stress to succeed built until he was consumed with shame. He was ashamed he wasn't doing as well as his peers or the bar that he had set for himself.

Now I'm not saying that's what will happen to you, but I think we need to consider what is really driving our success so that when work gets hard and we want to give up, we have a bigger reason than ourselves not to throw in the towel.

I felt a similar pressure when I was sixteen. The father figure who I had come to know for eleven years left my mom, my three sisters, and me.

The pressure to succeed and help my family started there. It was then that I decided I never wanted my family to have money problems again. At fourteen, I started working to help my family. I started picking blueberries for a local farmer for $10 an hour. In the summer, I got another job working for a landscaping company every Saturday. I got a third job a few months later working at Subway two to three times a week. I began to support myself and help my family whenever I could. I bought my own lunch, sports equipment, and kept up my 82' Chevy Pickup when I got my license.

Working so much at that age was hard. It wasn't an ideal situation. I probably would have rather been hanging out with friends or playing basketball, but I was motivated by helping my family. There's nothing I wanted more than to be able to help my mom and sisters. Sacrificing my own comfort for my family's wellbeing was what drove me to get out of bed every day. I worked hard for them, and found that the concept of being generous with my time and money was a greater driver for success than my own personal success could have ever been.

I realized my motivation for success was actually *generosity*, the desire to serve the needs of others, not my own achievement or money.

Two Types of Motivation

A motivation is the impulse that causes someone to act. When it comes to why we do the things we do, science shows there are two ways humans are motivated. We can be motivated intrinsically(internally) or extrinsically (externally).[21]

Internal motivators are why people create art, because something inside of them, an internal motivator, drives them to create objects filled with beauty and meaning. They don't create to make a bunch of money or to become famous, although some end up making their fortune and gaining fame. Artists create because they love it and it is personally rewarding.

An external motivator is an outward force that causes us to act. These are motivators we see almost every day. Here are a few examples of external motivators:

- A child cleaning his room to avoid being punished by his parents
- A salesman making more calls because her boss offered a trip to Paris to the team member with the highest sales.
- An athlete getting a bonus for helping his team reach a certain number of wins.

Likewise, when sales managers today offer bonuses and incentives to their salespeople, that is an example of an external motivator.

It is important that we can recognize these motivators in our own life. What is motivating you to reach the next level in your business? Is the motivator internal or external? Are you working for the incentive such as a new car? Or are you working because you love what you do and want to get better at it?

Which type of motivation will keep you motivated the most when things get hard? Will it be the internal reward or the promise of a new, big screen TV?

I think the scientific results will surprise you.

The Candle Problem

In 1962, a psychologist named Sam Glucksberg, working with the U.S. Army Human Engineering Laboratories, modified an experiment called the "Candle Problem.²²"

Individuals were led into a room that had a table in a corner. On the table were: a box of tacks, a candle, and matches. Their task was to attach the lit candle to the wall in a way that the wax wouldn't drip onto the table. Participants tried tacking the candle to the wall with no luck. Others tried to attach it with hot wax to the wall, but still failed.

This wasn't a new experiment. Another famous psychologist had published it years before. However, what Glucksberg did differently was that he separated his participants into two groups and gave *one* of those groups an incentive.

The first group was told that the person who solved the problem fastest would receive $20 (about $150 in 2015 dollars with inflation). Also, the top 25 percent who solved the problem fastest would receive $5 ($40 in 2015).

In Glucksberg's second group, they were not given an incentive. They had the same problem, same goal, but no external reward to solve the problem.

Eventually, almost all the participants figured out the correct way to solve the problem. First, empty the box of tacks, then tack the box to the wall, and place the candle on top of the box now affixed to the wall.

The question was, which group solved the problem faster?

In other words, which works better to motivate salespeople: A big screen TV, plus a new car, plus a vacation to the Bahamas? Or *nothing at all*.

On average, the first group, who was promised a cash reward, solved the problem three and a half minutes *slower* than the other group. To my surprise, the group with *no* external motivator actually solved the problem faster.

While it may seem they would help us work harder, external motivators, actually limit our creative thinking and problem solving.

As a team leader, I stopped throwing big screen TV's at my team members a long time ago. I began asking the members of my team what is motivating them. The two main consistent answers I got were: family, and proving to myself that I can do better. So I don't reward my team with electronics or trips to exotic places. I help them remember the things that are really motivating them. Rewards are nice, but they create a work-ethic based solely around external rewards. So when the TV isn't there, will you keep pressing into discomfort or give up?

This is why our internal motivator is the more important motivation. The candle problem is an example of how we often solve problems better when we *want* to solve them, not when someone tells us they'll give us something in return.

As a financial advisor, my job is to solve people's money problems, to help them invest right, and plan for the future. I have found that I do my best, most effective work when my clients have problems I *want* to solve.

How to Treat Your Clients with Generosity

There is a principle in business called, *sowing and reaping.*[23] It is the idea that before we can reap the benefits of success, we need to first sow the seeds that will actually get us there. We often approach business the other way around though. We feel pressure to make a lot of money, and be really successful when we start, but we rarely think and do the hard work of sowing the seeds that will help us get there and to continue growing our business.

I think you'll see through my experiences and the stories of others, that to achieve our full potentials, we actually need to learn to give. The principle of sowing and reaping is essential to our success. If we don't plant the seeds and do the hard work, we can never reap the benefits of *real, lasting* success. I believe the seeds of success are the seven mindsets. They are the foundation of success, because without them you will not be successful.

I naturally learned to be motivated by generosity because of my childhood situation. After going through a time of need, I realized how important it is to be generous to others when I could. This carried into my adult life and I have been able to be generous in ways I never imagined I could be. When I heard someone I cared about didn't have money for the something they needed, I made sure they were taken care of. When I heard that a family member didn't have a car they needed to get to work, I sacrificed to help.

Generosity to me means that I can hold my possessions loosely and have my mind open to opportunities to serve others.

As I integrated this generosity mindset into my business, I realized it was part of the reason I reached such a high level of success in such a short period of time.

In being generous, I have actually accomplished the "blue ocean strategy".[24] The blue ocean is about *creating* your own market (blue ocean), versus trying to compete in the traditional highly competitive market (red ocean).

In a business, like financial services, that can become easily commoditized, it matters what we are doing differently than the guy down the street. We can sell the same things, offer the same services, but what sets us apart?

The answer to that question for me has been *generosity.* When I first started my firm, I began to go above and beyond in ways my clients never expected but greatly appreciated. I've called banks for clients, finding which ones in the area could give my client the loan they needed, sat in on meetings with accountants, and connected my clients to real estate agents in the area.

Each time I did something like this, my clients were always extremely surprised. It was in these moments I realized that very few advisors in the business treat their clients like this. It was part of what separated me from the other advisors in the business, how generous I am with my time and resources.

In five years, my client isn't going to say, "Wow I'm really glad Sten bought that Vanguard fund over that Fidelity fund and earned us a half percent more." Although that's important and I'm here to help them make the best financial decisions, they are more likely going to remember that when they first moved to the city I helped interview three realtors and then connected them with the one that could help them find a home.

It's all about relationships. My clients aren't going to find another firm after I've shown them that I will go the extra mile for them.

When I meet with my team, I always ask them, "What separates us from the other advisors? Are we doing the same thing that those advisors are doing and hoping that we get a better result somehow?" There has never been a time that I regretted being generous with my time or resources.

Initially, I was generous out of habit. But after a few years, I saw that the more generous I was, the more success I had. Now, not only am I able to help serve others better, but helping others often ends up helping me as well. The clients I am most generous towards often end up being lifelong clients that refer even more business to me. Even better, generosity like this feels great and keeps me motivated to continue to do my job at a high level.

The needs of others play a significant role in each decision you make.

"Your true worth is determined by how much you give in value than you take in payment," says Bob Burg and John David Mann in the book, *The Go Giver.* In other words, the better you serve your clients and the more value you add to their lives, the more successful you'll be.

"Your income," the authors continue, "is determined by how many people you serve and how well you serve them." Your success is directly tied to the number of people you are serving.

You won't have a business success—or any kind of success— if you are not basing the decisions you make from the needs of your clients. You need to be generous and willing to hear what your clients really need. Generosity and the ability to solve other people's problems is what will keep you motivated on the long, hard days and far into the future.

Don't Have a Zero-Sum Mentality

There's this competitiveness in sales that has a "defend your territory" mentality. In economic theory, this mentality is called a Zero-Sum Game, a situation where if someone else wins, you lose, when someone else closes a big deal, it was actually *your* deal that *you* missed out on.

The truth is there are always more clients out there. This can be hard to believe when you're new to the business and don't know where to find new clients or customers. But the more time I've spent in this business, the more I realize there are always more great clients out there. This concept is true in any business. There will always be people looking to buy houses, insurance, cars, tech products, pharmaceuticals, and so on. In my case, there will always be people who need financial services. This is why generosity is so important. When we look at everyone as our competition, we can become closed off and skeptical of others around us, the opposite is true of generosity.

This is why I train and help other advisors in the business, because I believe what we need in this business is not *less* competition, but more good advisors who care about helping their clients. There will always be more business. If you buy into the belief that life is a Zero-Sum Game, you will find you are only hurting your success.

Motivation, Calling, and Your Success

You need something else to motivate you besides the money and the accolades. When you balance your checkbook and put the awards on the shelf, if that was all you wanted, you come to find that you still lack purpose and fulfillment. I know this because I've experienced it myself. Sure, I can buy a nicer car and a bigger house, but at the end of the day, I go home to my wife and kids and they are what really matters.

I've experienced adversity and struggled to pay my bills. As a teenager, the way we got out of financial hardship was by being generous with our time and sharing our resources as a family. When I was just building a business, and my wife and I had a hard time just getting by, the main reason I started gaining clients so rapidly was my desire to help them and my willingness to be generous with my time.

Depending on your definition of success, your journey will look different. But at the end of the day, you'll need something to keep you going on difficult days.

I am motivated by serving my clients the best I can and being able to help them. I am also motivated by being able to use my income to help others in my family and other good causes

This journey of becoming successful is sometimes given a bad reputation. It can come across as selfish, and if you are motivated by the money and proving other people wrong, I do think you'll end up ten years down the road wondering if this is where you wanted to be in the first place. Did you choose this because you love it and know you can make a difference in the lives of others? Or did you choose it because you could make a lot of money?

Look back to your definition of success. True success is waking up motivated by doing what you love and not having an impact simply on yourself, but the world around you. Honestly,

I don't think something is really worth doing if it doesn't in some way help someone else.

In our final chapter, we're going to talk about next steps as you apply these mindsets to your business. However, as you reflect on how to apply these seven mindsets to your life, keep in mind this principle of generosity. If the mindsets are the *how* behind success, I believe you'll find that generosity is the *why*, the motivator behind your success.

Generosity in Action:

In your next meeting with a client, be generous with the time and resources you have. Try going above and beyond for your client. The results you see from this might not be immediate, but they will change your business.

The seven mindsets are the tools that will lead you to success. You are behind the wheel, steering your success in the right direction, but one day you may wake up and find that you're sick of driving. You might even feel that way right now. You'll doubt your final destination and want to settle for where you are. In the last chapter, we'll look at these mindsets in action and determine once and for all, "Will you do it?"

Conclusion

It is not our abilities that show what we truly are. It is our choices.

—J.K. Rowling

This book has given you almost everything you need to know to be successful. These mindsets will change the way you see the world and the way you see success. They will equip you to reach your full potential in your business and all other aspects of your life.

Creating new mindsets is about seeing the world differently. Each mindset is like a different set of lenses in a pair of glasses. Each lens helps you see a new perspective, another way to improve your chances of success.

You never *arrive* at success, just as you can never fully achieve your full potential. It is something that is always growing, always expanding. It is a journey more than a destination. You will develop more into your full potential every day. As you put the seven mindsets to practice, you will learn more about your safety net, circumstances, discomfort, future self, conflict, time balance, and perspective. When you begin to see each day as an opportunity to get closer to your full potential, you will find more purpose and fulfillment in your success.

You'll never regret trying to reach your full potential. You might, however, wake up one day and regret *not* trying. I meet people every day who never bothered. They're fifty and in the same place they were when they were twenty-five. Somewhere along their journey, they settled for what they had and started to believe that better was outside of their control. I think you're reading this because you believe that you can still do more to achieve your full potential.

Your time and potential are too valuable to waste. Becoming intentional with each day will help you avoid waking up one morning and realizing you've been in the same place for the last ten years. Regret is a terrible feeling, and I want to do everything I can to help you avoid the costly mistake of not trying to reach your full potential.

In the pursuit of your full potential, I think you'll find that success naturally follows. When customers and clients see that you are striving to be the best realtor, financial advisor, or salesman that you can be, they will trust you more, and in turn you will earn more.

The Seven Mindsets in Action

I don't believe you can be successful without putting these mindsets into practice. Although they might not know it, some of the most successful people in the world have learned and adopted these mindsets.

Bill Gates[25] didn't create a company that immediately leapt off the ground. He first created something called Traf-O-Data, a device that was supposed to read traffic reports and data to help traffic engineers reduce road congestion. Believe it or not, the product didn't take off.

Soon after that, Gates contacted a company that had been building mini-computer kits, the predecessor to the personal computer, and claimed he had built an operating system that could run the computer. He was lying. He hadn't built the software, wasn't sure he *could* build the software. But he wanted to get their attention and he succeeded. In two months, he developed the software and brought it to the company. The software worked, and slowly Gates and his business partner Allen began to build the company that would later be known as Microsoft.

In this situation, Gates was the perfect embodiment of the seven mindsets.

- He made decisions based from his future self.
- He pursued discomfort, contacting a company about developing a new software.
- He got perspective from his business partner and friend.
- He removed his safety net by dropping out of Harvard to pursue a career in an unproven industry.

- He then controlled his circumstances by deciding to start his own company.
- We've seen various conflicts that Gates has dealt with in the news against companies like Apple, claiming that he infringed their copyright, and by dealing with that conflict, a judge ruled that the claims weren't true.
- All the tasks that he did as a CEO are wrapped up in intentional time balance and incredible delegation.

Whether knowingly or not, Bill Gates lived out the seven mindsets.

If Gates neglected to plan for the future, his company would become irrelevant, as technology changes so rapidly. If he avoided uncomfortable situations, he would never have taken the risk to start another company. If he kept his safety net, he could probably have lived in his parent's basement a few more years. If he never took hold of the circumstances he could control, he would have never had enough energy to focus on the thing he was really good at. If he had avoided conflict, his company could have ended up bankrupt. If he had managed time poorly, he would never have been able to run such a large, successful company.

When you look closely at the most influential people in the world, you'll find that most of them follow the seven mindsets. From the Wright Brothers to J.K. Rowling, successful people have a deep desire to reach their full potential and use the mindsets to help them get there.

You Drive Your Success

If you have these mindsets, you will be able to more clearly identify the road to success. The mindsets will serve as a guide to get you there through intentionality. You don't have to be pushed around by the industry and other advisors, while learning from your mistakes. This isn't about putting a bunch of principles into practice and hoping that they work. These mindsets are intentional tools that put you in the driver's seat of your success.

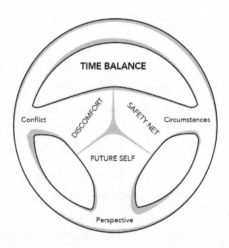

That is why we based the model of our diagram off of a steering wheel. The mindsets that make up the wheel are the tools that enable you to reach your destination. You really can be in the driver's seat. Realizing you are in control of your success is one of the biggest mindset shifts you need to make.

If you take hold and begin using these seven mindsets on your journey to success, you will be successful.

Will You Do It?

The last question is the one that will either get you off the couch, or cause you to make the conscious decision to settle for what you have now.

The last question isn't *can you* do these things and be successful, it's, *will you?*

Will you do it?

There may have been times while reading this book where you felt overwhelmed and defeated. The concepts in this book can sound like a lot, especially all at once, and I realize that. It is so important that you not let yourself be defeated when reading them, because you really are in control.

The benefit of the seven mindsets will last your entire life, and not only will they affect your business, but your personal life as well.

Removing your safety net will help you reach higher, swim deeper, and achieve more than you think you can. Imagining your future self will give you a clear picture of where you want to go, so you can actually figure out how to get there. Embracing discomfort will grow you faster and further than holding onto your comfort will. Getting perspective will enable you to avoid mistakes that others before you have already made. Focusing on the circumstances you can control will help you use your limited time and energy more efficiently on the things that are really working. Embracing conflict will allow you to develop much deeper relationships and be more trusted by your clients. Balancing your time will allow to you to live effectively and intentionally.

Years ago, I was faced with the decision to stick with a comfortable job that paid me well, or risk everything and start my own firm. I looked at my future self and knew I didn't want to be in the same place in ten years. I chose discomfort and changed my circumstances to see if I could achieve success. Every day since then I've had to embrace conflict and seek perspective when it would have been easier not to, but in only three years I've built a successful business, in a crashing economy. My income has doubled every year for the last three years. My business is growing rapidly, and not only am I offering services and products to my clients, but I am serving them *well.*

We call the kind of success we're aiming for "Rapid, Top-Level Success" for two reasons: your success shouldn't be cheap like a dingy car with a new paint job, or a gold-plated engagement ring. "Top-Level" success is like the highest-quality luxury car, a solid gold wedding ring. The "Rapid" part of your success comes from being laser-focused with your time. Instead of wasting twenty years waiting for business to take off, you can take control of the time you have and are able to amplify and speed up the process.

The more you practice these mindsets, the easier they will become. After embracing discomfort for years, I'm no longer scared or anxious each time some new, uncomfortable task comes up. The longer you adopt and implement these mindsets in your life, the more change will come, and the closer you will get to your full potential. You'll start meeting your goals and the success you always envied will be in your grasp.

My definition of success is different now than three years ago. It's different than it was one year ago too. What I use to measure my success changes too—before, it was just my income, but now I'm focused on the success of my team members as well.

With that being said, changing your mindsets and embracing these concepts is going to be hard and uncomfortable. But if your sole purpose is comfort, you will never be successful. If you never take a risk, you're never going to get any closer to your goal. Sure, some people have been successful simply by being in the right place at the right time. But are you going to leave your future up to chance?

In fact, I believe anybody can do this. Anyone can do what I have done, and even more. You just need to know where to start and what the map looks like. In the same way, most people can cook a great meal when given the right instructions and ingredients, almost anyone can be successful with the right guide. Let these mindsets be your guide.

Now that you've read this book, I believe you have an obligation to do something. Your mind has been opened to these principles and it's your job to implement them in some way in your life.

Not can you, but will you?

If you choose not to, you'll look back and say, "I missed out. I should have tried when I had the chance."

The comfort in avoiding these mindsets will be temporary, but the results and growth that comes from embracing these mindsets will last your entire life.

I don't want this to be like another New Year's resolution that lasts for a few weeks and then you forget about it. I want this to be a life changing way of seeing yourself and the world around you.

If you are willing to do what it takes to be successful, then go do it.

Don't forget about the journey between what you want and your goal. It's easy to look at where you are now and where you want to be in five years, but unless you also imagine the time in between, you will end up in the same place.

Consider what it's going to take and if you're really willing to fully embrace the journey. It's worth it, I promise. You'll only regret never trying.

Take Your Success
to the Next Level, Today

Congratulations, you've taken the first step towards reaching Rapid, Top-Level Success.

But it doesn't stop here.

Online, I've compiled resources and practical tips that will help you reach your goals.

Follow the blog, download the free guides, and let the seven mindsets revolutionize your success.

Your future success is just a few steps away:

1. Head over to <u>stenmorgan.com/mindsets</u>
2. Enter your name and email in the space provided
3. Click "Submit"

You'll be on your way to achieving the success you always dreamed of.

You don't want to miss this.

About the Author

Sten Morgan graduated from Linfield College in Oregon with a Bachelors of Science in Finance and Economics. After college, Sten worked for a large, successful financial firm and became a top-selling advisor. Sten left that job to pursue his own business, started from nothing and built a successful company.

Since then Sten has won numerous awards. Among them, the 30 Under 30 award for millennials making a transformation in their industries, awarded by LifeHealthPro and the 30 in their 30's award for non-profit leaders in Tennessee. Most prestigious, he was one of the youngest advisors ever to receive the Chairman's Council in his industry this last year.

Sten currently lives in Franklin, Tennessee with his wife, Taylor and their two daughters.

For more resources and exclusive content, head over to www.stenmorgan.com.

Sources

1   "Success." Oxford Pocket Dictionary of English.
    Accessed February 22, 2016. https://www.google.com/
    search?q=define:success.

2   Merriam-Webster. Accessed February 22, 2016. http://
    www.merriam-webster.com/dictionary/mind–set.

3   "Learned Helplessness." Wikipedia. Accessed February 22,
    2016. https://en.wikipedia.org/wiki/Learned_helplessness.

4   "Top 5 Stressful Situations & Stressors in Life."
    HealthStatus. 2009. Accessed February 22, 2016. https://
    www.healthstatus.com/health_blog/depression-stress-
    anxiety/top-5-stressful-situations/.

5   "Change Is Hard, Here's Why You Should Keep
    Trying." Psychology Today. Accessed February 22, 2016.
    https://www.psychologytoday.com/blog/high-octane-
    women/201210/change-is-hard-heres-why-you-should-
    keep-trying.

6   "MINDSET." MindSet: A Book Written by Carol Dweck.
    Teaching a Growth Mindset Creates Motivation and
    Productivity in the Worlds of Business, Education, and

Sports. Accessed February 22, 2016. http://mindsetonline. com/.

7 "Stanford Marshmallow Experiment." Wikipedia. Accessed February 22, 2016. https://en.wikipedia.org/ wiki/Stanford_marshmallow_experiment.

8 "Marshmallow Test." The Atlantic. Accessed February 22, 2016. http://www.theatlantic.com/health/ archive/2014/09/what-the-marshmallow-test-really- teaches-about-self-control/380673/.

9 "You Make Better Decisions If You "See" Your Senior Self." Harvard Business Review. June 2013. Accessed February 22, 2016. https://hbr.org/2013/06/you-make- better-decisions-if-you-see-your-senior-self/ar/1.

10 "Maslow's Hierarchy of Needs." Wikipedia. Accessed February 22, 2016. https://en.wikipedia.org/wiki/ Maslow's_hierarchy_of_needs.

11 "Good Stress, Bad Stress - ULifeline." Good Stress, Bad Stress - ULifeline. Accessed February 22, 2016. http:// www.ulifeline.org/articles/450-good-stress-bad-stress.

12 "Stress Can Be a Good Thing If You Know How to Use It." Harvard Business Review. 2015. Accessed February 22, 2016. https://hbr.org/2015/09/stress-can-be-a-good- thing-if-you-know-how-to-use-it.

13 "George VI." Wikipedia. Accessed February 22, 2016. https://en.wikipedia.org/wiki/George_VI.

14 "Fear." HowStuffWorks. Accessed February 22, 2016. http://science.howstuffworks.com/life/inside-the-mind/ emotions/fear.htm.

15 "Perspective." Dictionary.com. Accessed February 22, 2016. http://dictionary.reference.com/browse/perspective.

16 "Johari Window." Wikipedia. Accessed February 22, 2016. https://en.wikipedia.org/wiki/Johari_window.

17 "Lebron James." ESPN. Accessed February 22, 2016. http://espn.go.com/nba/story/_/id/9825052/how-lebron-james-life-changed-fourth-grade-espn-magazine.

18 "Kyle Korver." Basketball-Reference.com. Accessed February 22, 2016. http://www.basketball-reference.com/players/k/korveky01.html.

19 "The One-Day-a-Year Fitness Plan." Outside Online. 2014. Accessed February 22, 2016. http://www.outsideonline.com/1928041/one-day-year-fitness-plan.

20 "Wright Brothers." Wikipedia. Accessed February 22, 2016. https://en.wikipedia.org/wiki/Wright_brothers.

21 "Motivation." University of Rhode Island. Accessed February 22, 2016. http://www.uri.edu/research/lrc/scholl/webnotes/Motivation.htm.

22 "The Candle Problem." Wikipedia. Accessed February 22, 2016. https://en.wikipedia.org/wiki/Candle_problem.

23 "The Go Giver." Wikipedia. Accessed February 22, 2016. https://en.wikipedia.org/wiki/The_Go-Giver.

24 "Blue Ocean Strategy." Blue Ocean Strategy. Accessed February 22, 2016. http://www.blueoceanstrategy.com/.

25 "Bill Gates." Wikipedia. Accessed February 22, 2016. https://en.wikipedia.org/wiki/Bill_Gates.

www.TheMorganJamesSpeakersGroup.com

We connect Morgan James published
authors with live and online events
and audiences whom will benefit
from their expertise.

Morgan James
Speakers Group

Morgan James makes all of our titles available
through the Library for All Charity Organizations.

www.LibraryForAll.org

Printed in the USA
CPSIA information can be obtained
at www.ICGtesting.com
JSHW082349140824
68134JS00020B/1974

9 781683 503019